I'Anson's Chalet on Headley Hill

A HIDDEN HOUSE – A HIDDEN HISTORY

For almost one hundred and thirty years, a house has perched hidden and secluded behind the trees on Headley Hill while enormous changes have taken place in the world. During the nineteenth century the industrial revolution changed rural England forever. Two world wars in the first half of the next century shattered an old world order, as well as a social class structure which had existed in England for centuries. Unimaginable strides in technology during the twentieth century brought life to an unrecognisable point from where it had been in the 1870s, when an architect named Edward I'Anson built a house he named *The Chalet*, the first house on Headley Hill.

The Chalet, alias Windridge, with the Trollope family in 1927

I'Anson's Chalet
on Headley Hill

A HIDDEN HOUSE – A HIDDEN HISTORY

Judith Kinghorn

In Memory of
SARAH DIANA BERGQVIST
of BENIFOLD, HEADLEY
1963 – 2003

See the world in a grain of sand
And a heaven in a wild flower
Hold infinity in the palm of your hand
And eternity in an hour.

I'Anson's Chalet on Headley Hill

First published 2004

Typeset and published by John Owen Smith
19 Kay Crescent, Headley Down, Hampshire GU35 8AH

Tel: 01428 712892 – Fax: 08700 516554
wordsmith@johnowensmith.co.uk
www.johnowensmith.co.uk

© Judith Kinghorn

ISBN 1-873855-48-6

Text printed and bound by Antony Rowe Ltd, Eastbourne

CONTENTS

LIST OF ILLUSTRATIONS

Introduction

In March 2001 my family became the owners of a house called *Windridge* in Headley, Hampshire. We had made the life-changing decision to leave London six months earlier, to leave modern urban living for a quieter, hopefully healthier and possibly simpler country life.

The house was originally called *The Chalet*, and was indeed built in the style of a Swiss chalet around 1880 by Edward I'Anson, a renowned architect, philanthropist and local landowner. For two or more decades no other property was developed around it, and it stood at that time entirely alone on Headley Hill, close to an area then known as "Little Switzerland".

My interest in the house's history began with the discoveries and questions arising during its refurbishment:– solid slate window sills found under decades of chipped and bubbled gloss paint, tiled hearthplaces suddenly exposed to daylight after decades in darkness and the original varnished Victorian wallpaper hidden underneath a century of layers of differing patterns and fashions.

All of this fired my curiosity, and once I had established who had built the house and when, I wanted to know the more intimate details about the its past. Who had lived here when it was new and modern? Who had climbed the staircase with a candle or oil lamp on their way to bed one hundred years ago?

I eventually found my cast of characters, not as ghostly shadows from the past but as vibrant and complex individuals who led truly fascinating and sometimes scandalous lives. It is these people who bring a house to life and permeate its atmosphere. The tiny and even mundane details of their day-to-day existence are often more fascin-ating than the broader social and economic history of the times, for this is what brings history into focus and give it shape.

I discovered that the people who lived here were predominantly women and, even more poignantly, women who had lived here on their own. For any woman to live alone in an area as rural as Headley in the late nineteenth and early twentieth century shows a certain courage, but also begs the question, why? They all seemed to have had one thing in common, a need to be alone in a secluded place, and all of them had suffered loss and disappointment in their lives. In some ways their stories resemble each other, and occasionally overlap.

Researching the history of one's home can become an absorbing passion because of the inevitable involvement with the characters who once lived in the house and with whom one is inexorably linked. It is impossible to anticipate just who we will meet during the course of our research, but whether we love them or loathe them, we will never be indifferent to them. Their lives are examined and scrutinised by us for clues to their character and habits, in an attempt to get to know and understand them and the era that they lived in.

Inhabiting a space – a house – once filled by another, no matter how long ago, seems to lend an intimacy and a perceived familiarity to the relationship. These people we seek to discover are not long-lost relatives, but neither are they creatures of fiction. They lived and breathed, laughed and cried, suffered and triumphed within the walls where we now do the same and continue the great cycle of life.

Judith Kinghorn
September 2004

Little Switzerland

In the late nineteenth century, an area then generally known as the Hindhead Hills became a very fashionable place. One of the people who helped this happen was Edward I'Anson[1]. His name is known today to many local historians and to architects, but he is possibly not as well-known amongst the residents of Grayshott and Headley as he could or should be.

In the late 1850s when I'Anson is said to have first visited the area, it was made up of a few scattered cottages, huts and "lawless folk". The predecessors of these squatters had been "runagates" – people who had fled from justice "and skulked like the badger or the fox" in the woodland and commons around the mist-shrouded and wild Hindhead Hills. Up until the mid nineteenth century, the Hindhead Hills had been a "no-man's-land" and a place where people would travel at their peril due to the notoriety of highwaymen and robbers who preyed on travellers between Portsmouth and London. It was perhaps safer at this time to make a detour avoiding Hindhead by going through the pretty village of Haslemere.

Rolston's well-known local history book "Haslemere 1850–1950" mentions I'Anson's early days in Grayshott and states that "Over in Grayshott" in the early 1860s "one or two families – including the I'Ansons – had settled in spite of the reputation for roughness which the hamlet then bore". There had been "much pauperism" and "some victims of the enclosures" and gangs of men "marauded, robbing and terrorising travellers, stealing sheep and stock from local farms".

Hindhead and the surrounding area only became accessible and ripe for development after the railway arrived at Haslemere in 1859. It was then that wealthy Victorians began to travel down from London, where tuberculosis had taken hold and where the ever-present smog filled the

---

[1] The 'discovery' of Hindhead is usually credited to Professor Tyndall, but according to Thomas Wright who wrote "Hindhead or the English Switzerland" in the late 1890s, Mr Edward I'Anson "was also largely instrumental in causing the place to become a famous health resort".

city air. Londoners in the late nineteenth century came to Hindhead and the surrounding area known as "Little Switzerland" for its clean 'alpine' air and to walk in the natural wilderness – looking for the promise of 'good health'.

The arrival of new Victorian wealth in the area heralded an era of great investment and development within the settlements around Hindhead. One place to benefit from this "new money" was the village of Grayshott which was beginning to take shape at the same time that Hindhead became established. High above sea level and surrounded by dramatic and untamed heathland, it too had panoramic vistas, woodland walks and the clean air so sought after.

During the 1880s and 1890s many hotels sprang up in and around Hindhead – such as Moorlands, Thorshill (which later became the Devil's Punch Bowl Hotel), The Beacon Hotel, Glen Lea and The Royal Huts[2].

The Huts at Hindhead, circa 1890

The area inevitably became more civilised as people like I'Anson established homes there and took a committed interest in it, and subsequently invested in its development and future. It was he who established the early infrastructure for the modern village of Grayshott and the school, which like so much else in early Grayshott was built and funded by the I'Ansons and opened in 1871 with just one classroom, was its first public institution – before the Church, before the Village Hall and before the public house.

---

[2] The Huts had been a coaching inn from the early 1800s, and was mentioned by William Cobbett in November 1822 when he found himself near some "buildings called the Huts" in an area he did not like and had tried his best to avoid. The site was redeveloped during 2002 as a housing estate.

In fact the school became the social centre of the village, being the venue for many local events and evenings of music and entertainment of which the Victorians were so fond. Before this time children in Grayshott were expected to walk to the school in Headley, almost three miles away, and the consequential truancy and lack of attendance from the children of Grayshott is hardly surprising.

Crossways Road, Grayshott, 1901

At about the same time, Grayshott had its first shop at *Mount Cottage* (now *Hunters*).   This eventually moved in 1877 into a purpose-built building in Crossways Road, again funded by the I'Ansons.   Here the village post office opened some ten years later. Before this time the post had been delivered to the I'Anson home at *Heather Lodge* and distributed from there.

It was into this developing area with its picturesque landscape that many artists, writers, naturists and modern-thinkers moved, looking for inspiration – away from the stress, smog and hubbub of the city, but close enough to travel back when needed.

Professor John Tyndall, scientist and mountaineer, the first man to climb the Matterhorn in 1860, was one of these newcomers and someone whose love of Switzerland took him and his wife Louisa on regular trips to the Alps each year.   Around 1880, twenty years after Edward I'Anson had moved to Grayshott, Professor Tyndall came to live in Hindhead.   His deteriorating health meant that he was no longer able to travel to his beloved Switzerland, so the area which was to become known as "Little Switzerland" was the closest England could offer him.   By the mid-1880s Hindhead had developed into a thriving community and a recognised health resort, with a choice of good-quality hotels.

Victorian artists and writers firmly believed that being close to nature and wilderness aided the creative process, and together they formed a colony, a sort of Bohemia in "Little Switzerland". Some of the most influential figures in Victorian literary Britain set up home here on the Surrey–Hampshire border – these included Lord Tennyson, Mrs Gaskell, George Eliot, Lewis Carroll, James Barrie, George Bernard Shaw, Arthur Conan Doyle and HG Wells among many others. The area's relative proximity to London, then the centre of the publishing world, together with its peace and rural quality made the proposition of moving here appealing for creative thought as well as commercially advantageous.

Devil's Punch Bowl, Hindhead at the start of the 20th century

Thomas Wright describes the area in 1898:

"We had often heard of Hind Head – the English Switzerland – with its multitudinous pines, its miles of purple heather, its village eight hundred feet above sea level – far and away the loftiest settlement, one would suppose, not only in England, but in the British Isles – its wonderful Devil's Punch Bowl, peopled with a picturesque race of aborigines who get their living by the poetical fashion of working the landscape into brooms; we had heard of Hind Head, the literary Olympus, the abode of so many cultured notables that some wag felicitously suggested that the name should be altered to Mind Head"

He also commented *"Hind Head, of which Grayshott is only a part, is now one of the most fashionable health resorts within forty miles of London"*.

The I'Ansons

Edward I'Anson was born in London on July 5th 1811 and was the first child of five, the son and heir of another Edward I'Anson who was a reputable London-based architect. Edward followed in his father's footsteps becoming a prominent architect of his day, and President of RIBA (the Royal Institute of British Architects) from 1886 until his death in 1888. His works include the Royal Exchange Buildings (1842–44) and many office buildings in the City of London, as well as St Bartholomew's Hospital (1878–79) and the school of the Merchant Taylors Company at Charterhouse, the British & Foreign Bible Society, and the Corn Exchange in London (1881).

At the time of building the Royal Exchange, the construction of buildings to be used exclusively as offices was in its infancy and it was Edward I'Anson who is credited as the pioneer of this concept.

Edward was educated mainly in France at the Collège Henri Quatre and afterwards spent a number of years travelling extensively in Europe to France, Germany, Italy, Greece and Turkey. During these travels he made detailed drawings and notes which he used in later years and which gave him an artistic interpretation.

Royal Exchange, London

In June 1842, at the age of thirty-one, he married Catherine Blakeway and together they produced seven children, five daughters and two sons. All of Edward and Catherine's children took their mother's maiden name, Blakeway, as their middle name and their eldest child, Edward Blakeway I'Anson, followed the family tradition and also became an architect.

Though not as recognised or successful as his father, Edward Blakeway I'Anson worked with him for many years and eventually took over his father's practice at 7a Laurence Pountney in the City.

It is long recorded, and almost a part of local folklore, that Edward I'Anson rode down on horseback from Clapham Common to Grayshott in 1861 to look at the estate of some 73 acres known as "Grayshott Park" which he subsequently purchased for £137. It was on this land that he built his grand mansion *Heather Lodge*[3] in 1862.

Although a successful and established architect in London and a man of means, Edward I'Anson was also a humble and deeply religious man. In 1864, barely two years after moving to Grayshott, his daughter Lavinia Blakeway I'Anson died at the age of fifteen and two years later his wife Catherine died at only forty-six years old. Catherine and Lavinia are both buried at Norwood cemetery but some years later Edward commissioned a stained glass window in their memory in All Saints' Church, Headley.

I'Anson, then in his fifties, divided his time between his house at Number 5, The Terrace, Clapham, London where he lived during part of the week, and his mansion in Grayshott where he stayed at weekends and holidays. During 1867 and 1868 he visited Russia and subsequently wrote a paper on his visit which he read to a packed lecture theatre at RIBA.

In 1872, six years after his wife's death, Edward's elder daughter Mary married a Swiss banker from Neuchatel named David de Pury, who owned *Grayshott House* on the corner of the lane to Waggoners Wells. Mary and David de Pury continued to live there but also maintained very close ties with the de Pury family in Switzerland, enjoying regular visits to them.

---

[3] *Heather Lodge* was situated behind what is now the Catholic church and the house later became known as *Grayshott Court*. After his father's death in 1888, Edward Blakeway I'Anson sold the house to Mr and Mrs Vertue and *The Court* became a centre for the Catholic community in the area. In 1912 Mrs Vertue, by then a widow, gave the house to the Order of Our Lady of the Cenacle and it became the Convent of the Cenacle. Between 1914 and 1918 the Convent was used as a military hospital. Sadly, the Convent was demolished in 1999 and is now a private housing estate.

Edward I'Anson, 1811–1888

From the time of Mary and David's marriage[4] various members of the I'Anson family visited Switzerland, and perhaps it was these visits that inspired Edward to build his own Swiss chalet in Hampshire. However, he had already travelled a great deal in Europe, particularly to Switzerland and Italy as a young man.

In 1874, Edward's daughter Harriet married Cecil W.E. Henslowe and they moved into the newly built *Pinewood* in Grayshott, where they lived for many years. Both of Edward's daughters were married in the Parish Church at Clapham Common, where they had been members of the congregation as children growing up in London.

Sadness blighted Edward's life again on August 14th 1875, when his eighteen year old daughter Isabel Clara died. Her loss must have been painful for Edward, then in his mid-sixties, and it was around this time or shortly afterwards that he became close to Caroline Shepherd who had lived in Rome for many years of her life[5].

Caroline was twenty years younger than Edward, who became her third husband, and is described in Bryan I'Anson's book about the I'Anson family as "a relict of the Comte de Champs". She did indeed call herself Caroline, Countess de Champs I'Anson later in life, but many years of her life remain a mystery, particularly those spent overseas.

Edward, having been alone for more than a decade, decided to marry Caroline sometime in or around 1876, possibly in England although no record of their marriage has been found. His children were by this time grown up, in their twenties and thirties, and one can only speculate on their thoughts at their father's attachment to someone

---

[4] In 1895 Mary and David's daughter Berthe married Alexander Ingham Whitaker (known affectionately as 'Ninghy') whose family had bought the Wishanger estate and owned much of the land in the area. In fact at the end of the 19th Century most of the land in the area of Grayshott and much in Headley was owned by either the Whitakers or the I'Ansons. Berthe and Alexander lived at Grayshott Hall for almost thirty-three years up until 1928 and in the late 1890s they commissioned Edward Blakeway I'Anson, Berthe's Uncle, to design some quite grand additions to the house, including the tower.

[5] Caroline I'Anson's first husband, a Civil Engineer named James Shepherd, had died in 1862 while working on new buildings at the railway station in Rome, leaving her a widow with, at that time, four sons to bring up. In 1865 she married Antonin de Champs in Havre, France, but it is not known how long this marriage lasted – however presumably Caroline was left a widow for a second time.

almost the same age as they were.

It is noted in many architectural journals that Edward I'Anson spent November and December of 1878 living in Rome and it may be that this was when he either married Caroline or enjoyed a long honeymoon there with her subsequent to their marriage. Caroline had lived in Rome from 1858 for an undetermined number of years and so it may have been in Rome that Edward I'Anson met and later married her. The I'Ansons were certainly back in Rome during the winters of 1883, 1884 and 1885, and in May 1886 Edward gave a lecture at RIBA, as its President, on "Municipal Works in Rome". During the winters of 1882 and 1883 the I'Ansons also spent time in Cyprus, where Edward made many detailed drawings, now part of the collection at RIBA.

For the twelve years of their marriage, while in England, Caroline and Edward lived between their house in West London at 28 Clanricarde Gardens and *Heather Lodge* in Grayshott. However, it is interesting to note that *The Chalet* on Headley Hill was built around the time of their marriage – and that Caroline was to live at the house many years later, in the final years of her life. It may have been a wedding present for her from Edward. It was certainly a very pretty and even feminine house in terms of its style and decorative detail.

By purchasing the Grayshott Park Estate in 1861, Edward I'Anson had secured his place as one of the biggest private landowners in the area. He owned more than 70 acres of land in Grayshott and Headley and as the area became more fashionable he was able to sell off small pieces for development and, possibly more importantly, he was able to establish himself as a man of influence in the area.

When Edward I'Anson died on January 30th 1888, he was in his London home at Clanricarde Gardens recovering from an operation to remove a tumour. He had been in poor health for some time, but it was still a huge shock to his family, friends, colleagues at RIBA, and to the people of Headley who lined the route when his body was brought down from London to be buried at All Saints'. Although he had lived much of his life in London and had worked there all of his professional life, Headley held a special place in his heart.

He left a long and very detailed Will, outlining his wishes regarding the I'Anson "Trust Properties" and his possessions as well as very precise instructions to his two surviving sons on how he wished his second wife to be looked after upon his death. However his "Last Will and Testament" also states *"if I should die in London I desire to be buried at Norwood Cemetery either in the same grave in which my late wife Catherine Blakeway I'Anson and my children Lavinia and Isabel are buried or in a new grave immediately adjoining thereto but if I die at Grayshott aforesaid then I desire to be buried in the Churchyard of the Parish Church of Headley in the County of Southampton"*. Despite the fact that he died in London his body was brought to Headley. His Will also made clear his desire "that my funeral be conducted in the simplest manner … omitting all plumes, cloaks, bands and scarves".

The day of I'Anson's funeral was reported extensively in local papers and in many national papers, with senior representatives from RIBA as well as local gentry and ordinary folk in attendance. He was described as "beloved by all" and "a dear friend and benefactor" to the people of Headley and Grayshott. All businesses in Headley closed on the day of the funeral and people lined the roads in "profound sorrow on all sides". Edward I'Anson had indeed been a philanthropist, a benefactor to the local people and a pillar of the community. The reaction and outpouring of genuine grief at his death is testament to his standing in the community.

Among his many notable and charitable acts, Edward I'Anson had established and funded the school in Grayshott and his daughter Catherine Blakeway I'Anson continued the management of the school after his death. Catherine became a very prominent member of the community in Grayshott, mainly due to her commitment to the school, but with her brother Edward she also donated the land and funds for Grayshott to have its own church, St Luke's. Edward Blakeway I'Anson was the architect, who gave his services freely, and in 1901 Grayshott finally broke away from Headley to become its own ecclesiastical parish (and in the following year it also split away as a separate civil parish). Today the legacy of the I'Anson family to Grayshott is most evident in St Luke's Church.

Six months after his father's death in August 1888, Philip Blakeway I'Anson died at the age of forty-three at his home, *The Firs* (now *Beech Hill House*), on Beech Hill Road in Headley. It is not known how Philip died but he is also buried in Headley churchyard close to his father's marble tomb. It seems that he had never married. Philip's younger sister Emma, who outlived all of her siblings and lived in London, later named a plot of land in Grayshott after him, Philip's Green, now part of the Primary School grounds.

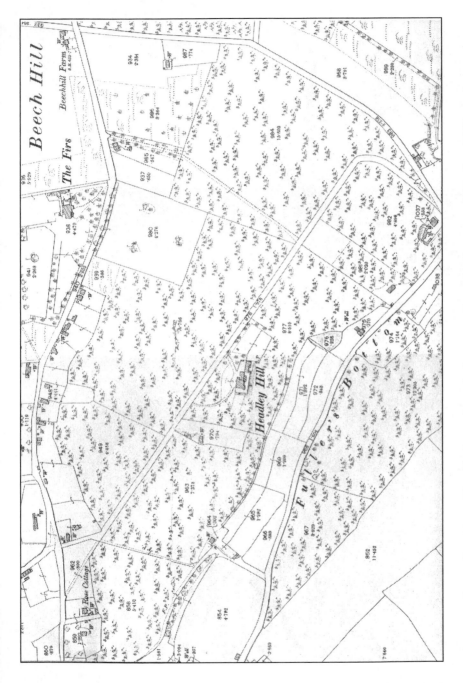

Headley Hill. 1895 – The Chalet is the only house and simply shown as 'Headley Hill' on the map

Headley Hill

It is due to Mr Laverty, the Rector of All Saints' in Headley, and his meticulously detailed notebooks that we know The Chalet on Headley Hill was built by Edward I'Anson, and the date of its construction can be narrowed down to between 1875 and 1881. The house is mentioned by Mr Laverty as early as 1882, when he notes "The Chalet on Headley Hill built by E. I'Anson" and a Mrs Vincent residing there – "a widow lady". Throughout Mr Laverty's notes over the fifty six years during which he was Rector, he refers to the house and its changing names and owners. A later reference by him explained that The Chalet was indeed a "Swiss Cottage".

The first map we have seen showing the house is the 1897 Ordnance Survey map where it is simply named "Headley Hill", and at this time it is the only house on Headley Hill. It does not appear on the previous series of OS maps dated 1871–1874.

Rev W H Laverty

The Chalet had been built on a hill overlooking a valley called Fullers Bottom and on the land where the famous "Fullers Earth" had been found. At the end of the winding road along the valley was the village green and beyond that the centre of Headley village, with its old church tower rising from the smattering of houses and cottages. Headley then was surrounded mainly by heathland, as its name implies. The house on Headley Hill was approached by a steep and narrow road which started at the "triangle" at the junction of Bowcott Hill and what is now Beech Hill Road, just above the hamlet of Arford. In the 1880s and 1890s there was no other practical way for a horse and carriage to access the house, though by foot one could also use the rough track leading up from Fullers Bottom (the "Cinder Track" as it was called because the holes in it were regularly filled with cinders).

Headley Hill, 1910 – The Chalet, here shown as **Heather Brow**, now has 'Pinehurst' as a neighbour

At 450 feet above sea level, secluded by pine trees, it would indeed have been reminiscent of Switzerland and very modern, even *avant garde*, in its day. Facing due south, with what were then described as "pleasure gardens" and woodland walks through the 8–10 acres of pine trees, it must have been an incongruous sight. When the house was first built it boasted seven bedrooms, three reception rooms, a Coachman's cottage, stables and two kitchen gardens as well as one of the first lawn tennis courts in the area. The Victorians had invented the mowing machine and with it came a love of lawns, beautifully manicured and tended, fit for the new game called tennis and, of course, croquet.

On the 28th December 1897, Mr Laverty recorded the following: *"It is to be noted that whereas the late Mr I'Anson some 15 or 16 years ago cut the new road (for the use of Headley Hill) through the small field numbered 873 on the Ordnance map of 1869, – he spoiled the original road 883 (on the same map) just beyond the upper end of his new road (through 873) which was made practically too steep for carts coming from the west end of No 888. Mr Bettesworth (guardian, etc) is said to have interviewed Mr I'Anson, on behalf of some cottagers, and to have obtained the promise that the new cut through 873 should remain open. This was told me in 1897 by James Marshall living at the west mouth of No 883, when Mr E.B. I'Anson closed the new cut, and I pointed it out to Mr E.B. I'Anson. He then opened the road again putting up notices that it was a Private Road. While it was closed the gates had been more than once broken open to allow of the passage of carts, which really had no other passage."*

In January 1899 Mr Laverty also noted: *"With reference to the Bridle Road which goes from James Marshall's past Mrs Aldred's past Headley Hill (Heather Brow) and ultimately down to near the head of Fullers Bottom – note that it much spoilt just above Mrs Aldred's (in the 80s) by the banking up required to make good Mr I'Anson's access through the little field. Mr I'Anson in 1897 or 1898 tried to close this road without making good the bridle path; but on remonstrance opened his road again."*

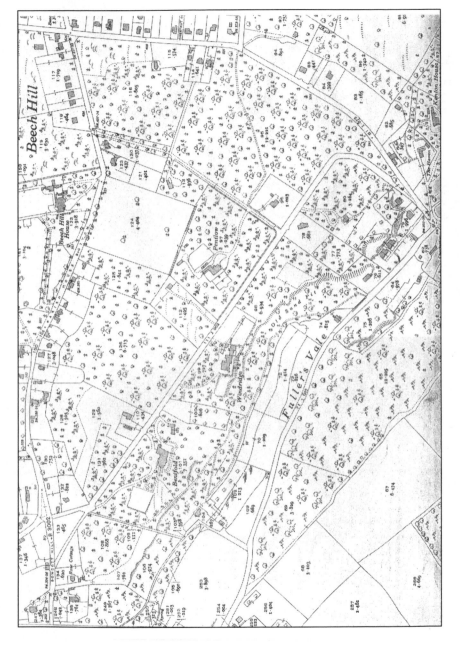

*Headley Hill, 1937 – the chalet, here called **Windridge**, with 'Pentlow, as a new neighbour*

The Chalet was built on a road which became known locally as "I'Anson Road" long before it was ever known as Headley Hill Road. It remains a private road and over the years there have been many disputes about right of way. Mr Laverty's notes about this matter in 1897 and 1899 confirm two other things; that it was indeed Mr I'Anson senior who built the house and laid down the road and that, according to his recollection of the date of the road, it had been built around 1881–1882, which would mean that the Mrs Vincent whom Mr Laverty mentions in 1882 was most probably the first person to live at the house.

Mrs Vincent

The Chalet, Headley Hill, 1882–1897

Charlotte Ella Vincent was the daughter of Joseph Godman, a gentleman landowner whose family had owned land in Surrey and Sussex for hundreds of years. Charlotte was the eleventh child of thirteen and was born in 1846 at Park Hatch, the family's estate at Hascombe, Surrey. The Godman family also had a house in Knightsbridge, London at 55 Lowndes Square.

Charlotte is always referred to in Headley records as "Mrs Vincent". She was the widow of Captain Francis Vincent of the Royal Navy and daughter-in-law of the Reverend Sir Frederick Vincent the Canon of Chichester, who had nine children from his first marriage and five sons from his second marriage.

Francis Vincent, a son of the first marriage, married Charlotte at St Peter's, Hascombe on 3rd January 1877. Their first child, a daughter named Evelyn Bertha was born on 14th October 1877, but sadly died at four months old. A second child, another girl, was born on 16th November 1878 and they named her Elsie Madeline.

They appear to have been living in Norfolk at the time of Elsie's birth but this must have been a very brief period of stability and happiness in Charlotte's early married life. When Elsie was barely eight months old, tragedy struck again when Francis died on June 28th 1879 aged only thirty-eight, probably from Consumption[6]. Within two short years Charlotte had been married, borne two children, lost a child and been widowed.

Charlotte's father, Joseph Godman had died in 1874 and so he never saw his daughter marry, but he would no doubt have been happy

---

[6] Consumption or Tuberculosis was so common a disease at this time that many London Hospitals would only open their doors from 2pm in the afternoon for an hour or two in order to admit new patients. It was also highly contagious and may have been the cause of their daughter Evelyn's death, eighteen months earlier.

with the match. Evidence of the Godman family's prominence in the community is still very visible[7], particularly at the church – St Peter's, Hascombe. There one can still see various plaques in honour of the family and a number of beautiful stained-glass windows dedicated from Charlotte and her sisters to their parents Joseph and Caroline. Outside the church under the shadow of a huge pine tree is Joseph Godman's imposing family vault, surrounded by the more humble headstones of other Godmans, including Charlotte's white marble tomb with Royal Navy insignia and her husband's name before her own. Close to Charlotte and Francis' grave is the small headstone of Evelyn, their four month old daughter.

The Vincent family seat was D'Abernon Chase at Ashstead in Surrey and they could match the Godmans in terms of wealth, land and status. The title of Viscount D'Abernon had been bestowed on the family in 1620 and in Debretts of 1882 it lists the "Reverend Sir Frederick of Stoke D'Abernon … Canon of Chichester, late Rector of Slinfold, born 8th January 1798".

Sometime in the late summer or autumn of 1882 Charlotte Vincent came to The Chalet, or Headley Hill as she preferred to call it, without a husband or parents, but with her surviving child Elsie and a servant named Sarah Davenport who had been with her at Park Hatch as Elsie's Nursemaid and who would loyally remain with them for the next two or three decades.

It was the only house on Headley Hill at the time and had about ten acres of land with it, although I'Anson owned most of the surrounding land – approximately another fifty acres. Charlotte took the house on a lease from the I'Anson family and lived at Headley Hill for the next fifteen years.

---

[7] The mansion that Joseph Godman had rebuilt in grand style for his family in 1851 burned down in a fire sometime before World War Two. It would be interesting to know exactly when Park Hatch's mansion disappeared from the landscape – this was a period when many of England's great houses disappeared either due to fires or demolition, as a direct result of the death duties then in place. During a ten year period no fewer than four hundred grand country houses disappeared from the English landscape. Park Hatch estate was owned by the Duke of Westminster until 1972, when he put the estate up for sale in 32 lots. Today the area of the old estate is still known as Park Hatch, but is divided into various farms and, of course, new houses.

Why Charlotte came to Headley, then a very rural place with few conveniences even by Victorian standards, is unclear. As a young widow in her early thirties and with a small child to look after, it seems a strange choice to have made. She arrived shortly after her mother's death on 28th June 1882[8], from her parents' estate at Park Hatch where

The road to The Chalet, 1899

she had been living since the death of her husband Francis three years earlier. Charlotte and her mother had lived in grand style there, with no fewer than thirteen servants in attendance including two footmen and a pageboy.

It does seem that Charlotte turned her back on life to an extent by coming here, away from the privileged life she had been born into and away from the sophistication of London and Park Hatch. By choosing the quiet confines of a rural village, any opportunity to meet an eligible husband and marry again would undoubtedly be limited, as would the opportunity to attend the balls and parties of her previous life. By coming to live in a small rural community, where much poverty and hardship were in evidence and where the church provided most of the entertainment, Charlotte at thirty-six years old chose to change her life considerably.

---

[8] Charlotte's mother, born in 1805, had 13 children and lived until she was seventy-seven years old. The family house in London at number 55 Lowndes Square in Knightsbridge and the estate at Hascombe were inherited by her elder brother upon the death of her mother who had been a widow for eight years. So it would seem that Charlotte probably had to move on and allow her brother and his family to move into their new home.

It is very possible that Charlotte decided to come to this area known as "Little Switzerland", with its clean alpine air and many sanatoriums, either because she or Elsie were consumptive or because she truly felt it would be a good preventative measure. There is evidence to suggest that Elsie was an invalid, which gives credence to this theory.

In 1882, Mr Laverty mentions a child named "Lily". This must have been Elsie and was no doubt her pet name, as she would have been only three years old at the time. Mr Laverty also notes another Miss Vincent "living at Headley Hill in 1883" and makes reference to a newspaper cutting attached to the same page of his notebook. This cutting, dated March 1883, is from *The Globe* Newspaper and outlines the will of the Reverend Sir Frederick Vincent who had died on January 9th. "Three daughters by the first marriage" which produced nine children including Charlotte's beloved Francis are mentioned, though not by name, and Mr Laverty refers to this article when he says "one of the daughters mentioned below", noting who was staying at the house with Charlotte.

So Charlotte Vincent was not after all entirely alone at this time and had one of her sister-in-laws living with her in Headley. The Miss Vincent mentioned is likely to be Isabella, the youngest of Sir Frederick's nine children from his first marriage. From Mr Laverty we know that Miss Vincent was still living at Headley Hill at Christmas 1884 when he appealed for help for George Harris of Whitmore Bottom – to replace his lost his pig. Donations were received from:

Laverty 5s
E Woodthorpe 2s
Miss Vincent 3s
Mrs Vincent 2s
Edward I'Anson 1s

Around Christmas in 1884, Mr Laverty noted that "Mrs Vincent is very anxious for us to have a new organ in Headley Church". This is not long after Charlotte's arrival in the village and shows that she very quickly became a committed part of the community through her faith and her connection to the church. In 1885 the new organ arrived funded mainly by Charlotte's generous donation of £100. Interestingly, the next highest donation was from Edward Blakeway I'Anson who gave £20, which certainly seems like a meagre offering compared to Charlotte's. However, Charlotte's donation confirms that she was certainly a lady of independent means, and with money from both the Vincent and the Godman families one can assume that she was very well provided for.

Two years later, in August 1886, Mr Laverty mentions that "E C

Howard Vincent and Mrs H V" are at The Chalet, which he says they "took furnished" from "half sister-in-law Mrs V". It would seem that Charlotte let her house to her brother-in-law for that summer, possibly in exchange for the use of his house at number 1 Grosvenor Square in London. It is highly likely that Mr and Mrs Howard Vincent were freshly back from one of their trips to some far-flung part of the British Empire.

Sir Howard Vincent[9] was the elder brother of Edgar Vincent, both sons of Sir Frederick's second marriage and so half brothers-in-law to Charlotte. It was Edgar who became a renowned and distinguished politician, diplomat and financier of his day and who also eventually became Viscount D'Abernon. Howard was also a politician, as well as an author and the cartographer responsible for producing the now famously decorative and colourful maps of Queen Victoria's Empire – which are still sold to this day. As MP for Sheffield Central, he and his wife spent time in the North but also travelled extensively, particularly within what was then the British Empire.

Howard's wife, Ethel Gwendoline, was the daughter and heiress of the MP George Moffatt and she wrote extensively of her various trips overseas with her husband. Together they visited China, North and South America, India and the West Indies among many other places.

Although the Victorians' love of travel and adventure is well documented, it was still unusual for a Victorian Lady to travel the globe by sea, in male company and with very few luxuries or comforts. Ethel Gwendoline Vincent was no casual observer however, and she wrote detailed accounts of her trips and her encounters with foreign lands and people. She had a number of books about her travels published during the 1880s and 1890s and although these now seem unbelievably naïve to the twenty-first century reader, littered with childlike and now politically incorrect observations, they remain a fascinating insight into how the Victorians viewed their Empire and other races and cultures around the world. Her publications include:

40,000 Miles of Land and Water – 1885
Newfoundland to Cochin China – 1892
China to Peru over the Andes – 1894

In August 1886, Mr Laverty mentions a "girl of three" at Headley Hill. This would have been Howard Vincent's daughter Vera, to

---

[9] C E Howard Vincent was knighted in 1896 and died in 1908 at the age of 59 years old. His wife Gwendoline lived in London at 42 Belgrave Square until her death, nearly half a century later, on February 14th 1952 at ninety-one years old.

whom Ethel Gwendoline dedicated her first book when it was published in 1885. The parish magazine of November 1886 states that "The Howard Vincent map of the British Empire has been kindly presented to Headley School by C.E. Howard Vincent Esq C.B., M.P." Howard Vincent and his wife were regular house guests at Headley Hill and so they would have become familiar to some of the other residents of Headley. It is also likely that they rented other houses in the area over the years, as they are mentioned much later by Mrs Hubbuck as dinner guests at *Pinehurst*.

It is a measure of the Vincent family, their achievements and prominence in society during the late nineteenth and early twentieth centuries that many of their family records, letters and documents are held by the Historical Manuscripts Commission and with the British Library and Oxford and Cambridge University Libraries.

Interior of All Saints' Church, Headley in 1908

Charlotte Vincent, like Edward I'Anson, was a notable member of the congregation at All Saints' Church in Headley at this time. She was quite obviously a deeply religious woman whose faith had been of comfort to her as a young widow, and she supported the church and the community in Headley in many ways. This is confirmed and detailed by Mr Laverty in his notebooks and by the Parish magazine, "The Monthly Illustrated Journal" (which was started by Mr Laverty in 1872), when her name appears regularly as a benefactor. If ever there was a cause, a collection or someone in distress, Charlotte always seemed willing and able to contribute.

Mr Laverty notes on 12th July 1889: *"Thomas Burrell has lost a cow worth £7–£8. In his enfeebled state of health this is to him a most serious loss and he appeals for aid to enable him to replace the cow."* Mrs Vincent donated 5 shillings.

Again Mr Laverty notes on 31st January 1890 that James Marshall has had an *"accident by which his cart and harness are very much broken his young horse considerably damaged"* "C.E.V." (Charlotte Ella Vincent) donated 2 shillings.

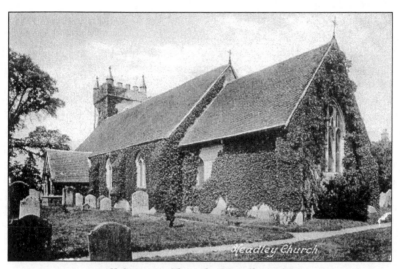

All Saints' Church, Headley 1901

On 28th April 1892, Mr Laverty details another sorrowful example of the poverty in rural England at this time: *"William Kemp has been seriously ill with pleurisy and has gone with one child to his mother's in Eastbourne. It is now thought better that his wife and other child should also go to Eastbourne. The expense of moving them and their furniture will be about £2 which after Kemp's long illness they are unable to find."* Mrs Vincent donated 2 shillings and sixpence.

There were many appeals like this by Mr Laverty during the 1880s and 1890s, and in all of these appeals for help Charlotte Vincent's name is prominent amongst the few who were able to contribute and her contributions were always some of the most generous.

She was also an accomplished pianist and, as an integral member of the community, joined in with many of the evenings of "entertainment" organised by the church and attended by Mr Laverty and Edward I'Anson among others.

Entertainment during this time usually included poetry recitals as well as music. The piano and music was almost mandatory to the Victorian house's "withdrawing" or drawing room. Oil lamps and gaslight which lit most middle-class homes made reading difficult so, especially after dinner, music and song were the order of the day along with cards, bridge and board games. At this time ladies in particular were expected to be accomplished in music, particularly at the piano, as well as in drawing and painting.

Charlotte Vincent and the I'Ansons would have seen each other regularly at All Saints' Church and at various social events in the locality. Of course Charlotte leased an I'Anson property and had lived in London for many years before moving to Headley, so it seems more than plausible that she would have known or met the I'Ansons on the social circuit in London, possibly in the late 1870s.

She certainly seemed to want to liven Headley up as Mr Laverty noted on July 2nd 1884: "The Club – started by Charlotte V", and goes on to give an account of its first meeting, which was at The Chalet but apparently without Mrs Vincent who was "not home at the time". Mr Laverty appeared shocked by the amount of beer and wine consumed at this gathering, as were some of his more abstemious parishioners. One can only wonder what Mrs Vincent thought afterwards – surely not what she had intended? However, we know the Club continued as Mr Laverty mentions it and some of the people involved in it later in his notes.

There are numerous recorded occasions when Charlotte herself took part in the "Entertainment" in Headley, usually organised by members of the Church community, and she would invariably play the piano, either solo or in a duet, and often with Mrs Kennedy who lived at Arford House. So we know for sure that the "withdrawing room" at Headley Hill housed a piano and that music was a part of Charlotte's life.

In July 1887, Queen Victoria's Golden Jubilee was celebrated in Headley with a "festival in the Rectory grounds" and was reported in the local papers and in the parish magazine of the time. The Garden Party at the Rectory was followed later in the day with a procession through Headley and finally "to Mrs Vincent's residence where the processionists were provided with light refreshments".

The refreshments provided would no doubt have been in the gardens of the house on that summer's day where the crowd would have been able to sit outside in Charlotte's well-tended grounds. Likely fare would have been beer and sandwiches, with lemonade for the children and Charlotte's loyal servant and Elsie's Nursemaid, Sarah

Davenport, as well as the Housekeeper, Mrs Louisa Elson, would have been on hand to serve. Fred Parham, the Gardener and one of six servants working at Headley Hill, would probably have been in the gardens on that day just as any other day. Fred lived with his wife and children in the small cottage between the stables and the walled garden. Louisa Elson's brother, James Robinson, also worked at the house as a Coachman and lived above the stables.

During the 1880s and 1890s, life for Charlotte must have been lonely and difficult at times, even in her comfortable position and living in what would then have been a new and very modern house, with servants on hand to see to most of her needs.

In 1896, Charlotte's brother Percy Sanden wrote and published a book which he rather humbly titled "Some Account of the Family of Godman" and in this he mentions Charlotte and Elsie living at "Headley Hill, Liphook". So Charlotte and her daughter lived at the house for at least fifteen years. Little "Lily", or Elsie, had grown up at Headley Hill and would have been a young lady of about eighteen years old when she and her Mother finally left the village sometime in the winter of 1897.

In fact Charlotte's departure from Headley Hill may have been due to another house being built nearby. At that time construction was about to start for the Hubbuck family on *Pinehurst*[10] just to the west of the Chalet, and this would undoubtedly have changed the landscape and impinged on Charlotte's solitude and privacy. One has to remember that Charlotte had grown up on her family's estate which covered hundreds of acres.

For whatever reason, late in 1897 Charlotte Vincent, her daughter and her loyal maid Sarah Davenport left Headley Hill for good and moved to a house called Cedar Lodge in Steeple Aston, Oxfordshire. Charlotte continued to live at Cedar Lodge with Elsie for the next twenty-one years until her death, two days after her seventy-third birthday, on 4th January 1919. She was buried at St Peter's, Hascombe on January the 8th alongside the husband she had lost forty years earlier, and close to their daughter Evelyn's grave. On Charlotte Vincent's tombstone are the words "Steadfast in faith", which seem to sum up her life – a life of widowhood, faith and compassion for others. Elsie was forty years old and without her mother for the first time in her life. In 1924 she sold Cedar Lodge, but it is unknown what happened to her from this point.

---

[10] Now *Benifold* – see later chapter.

The End of the Victorian Era

Victorian Britain can be viewed as a nation of double standards; the rich became richer with better food and living conditions, while the poor became poorer and often struggled to survive. The golden age of Victorian farming came to an end in England in the 1870s and a long depression set in, lasting for the rest of the century. The personal extravagance of the farmers was blamed almost as much as poor weather resulting in poor harvests, but it was the spread of the railways and the industrialisation of the country which changed farming and rural England forever. The railways attracted farm labourers with more money, better working conditions and better prospects, and from 1871 until 1911 the number of people in agricultural labour halved.

Headley High Street in the 1890s

During the time that Charlotte Vincent and the I'Ansons lived in Headley and Grayshott, the continual need for financial support for the poor from the local gentry highlights the enormous social divisions which existed and shows just how important the Church was in the community, particularly a rural community. The Church was a focal point, regardless of class or social status. The Industrial revolution had created "new money", but it had also destroyed rural communities and a way of life that had existed in England for centuries.

Headley in the late nineteenth century, like many other parts of rural England at this time, acquired some new rich residents who had found the perfect location for a country home. These "Nouveau riche" often built their country houses close to families living in appalling poverty and depravation. The newly elevated middle-class Victorians liked to fill their homes with servants, but almost more importantly with impressive new gadgetry and inventions as well as souvenirs from trips to different parts of the Empire[11].

However, some of those living comfortable lives seemed to have had a sense of moral obligation to help those less fortunate and it would appear that Charlotte Vincent, Edward I'Anson and the other affluent residents of Headley were genuinely compassionate people who did much good for their neighbours suffering hardship.

One of the rather quirky and unexpected consequences of the industrial revolution and the railways was the need for universal time. Before the coming of the railways each town or village had their own time, specified by the clock on the church or the town hall. But the railways changed that, and the solution became known as "railway time" with the station clock being the reference point for each town. Before that, each town and village in England operated to its own time, usually different from the next town or village and often very different from London time.

It is also true to say that the Victorians almost invented the internet, for when the telegraph cables were laid across the Atlantic and all the way to India it was the forerunner to today's cable traffic. So much of how we live today is as the result of Victorian invention: in fashion, morality and customs, sports, manners, gadgets, Christmas customs, social etiquette, roads, houses, bridges, trains and so much more.

---

[11] These were of course the same Victorians who were preoccupied with piety, social etiquette, appearances and personal virtue. It was an era when even piano legs had to be covered as they were deemed to be sexually provocative, and when the name of almost every "Bottom", including Fullers Bottom and Whitmore Bottom, was changed to "Vale" so as not to offend refined sensibilities.

The Calvert Sisters

Heather Brow, 1898–1911

Sometime in early 1898, after the departure of Charlotte Vincent, various additions were made to the house then generally known as *Headley Hill*, and this work was very probably carried out by Edward Blakeway I'Anson who had taken over his father's practice and who was also working on Grayshott Hall, his niece's home, a mile or so away. The work carried out at this time, almost twenty years after the house had been built, was very sympathetic and in keeping with the original chalet style, even down to the highly decorative drain pipes and guttering.

Shortly after this, two sisters moved in. Their names were Maud and Ida Calvert and their intention was to run a nursing home at the house, which they renamed *Heather Brow*.

The Census taken in March 1901 lists seven women living there: two are listed as "patient", another as "nurse/masseuse" and two who were sisters of seventeen and fifteen years old are listed as "servants". The head of the house, thirty-nine year old Ellen Ida Calvert is listed as "Hospital trained Masseuse/Nurse" and her thirty-four year old sister Maud Emily Calvert is a "Journalist/Writer". According to Mr Laverty's notebooks the house was indeed a nursing home run by the sisters whom he describes as "the two Miss Calverts". There were many sanatoriums in the area at this time, but this was the "first" in Headley – according to Mr Laverty.

However, by 1902, the Calvert sisters had already given up on their nursing home and thirty-five year old Maud, who was described as "literary" by Mr Laverty, had married a local man Cyril E. Fraser. Their wedding took place in June 1902 in Kensington, London which may well have been the original home of the Calvert sisters (the 1901 census gives their birthplace as Euston). At forty-three years old, Cyril finally left his mother's home, *The Chestnuts*, and nobly took over the lease of *Heather Brow*, rescuing the sisters from the financial burden of a twelve-year lease.

Edward Blakeway I'Anson, 1843–1912,
made sympathetic additions to the chalet in 1898

In the Cubitt and West ledgers of 1903 the house is listed as follows:

> 7 bedrooms, 3 reception rooms
> Dining room 18ft x 14ft
> Drawing room 30 ft x 14 ft
> Smoking room 16 ft x 14 ft
>
> 9 acres of Pinewood
> 2 large kitchen gardens
> Tennis lawn
> Stone/loose box etc
> Coachman's cottage

The newly-married Mr and Mrs Fraser never actually lived at *Heather Brow* themselves. The house was sub-let through Cubitt and West for many years and had a succession of tenants, mainly Army Officers stationed at Bordon Camp. The charge of 7 guineas "to let furnished for the winter" of 1903 is written in the Cubitt and West Ledger. It was let furnished for one year in 1905, to a Major Birch, by Bridgers in Haslemere, one of the few letting agents in the area at that time. In 1906 it was noted that "Mr Fraser would take £140 per annum" for the house and in the same year the ledgers mention that the lease has 4 years to run. At the same time it is noted that Edward Blakeway I'Anson was wishing to sell the property and was looking for £3,500 for the house. However some months later, despite not selling the house, it was recorded that "Mr I'Anson instructed that the price is £4,000 nett". In August 1906 it is noted that the house "is let to friends for a month – will be available again in September. Rent for winter months 4 guineas per week – includes gardener".

In June 1907 the house was let to Captain W.H. Walsh for 6 weeks at 9 guineas per week and after this a Mr Griffin rented the house for almost three years. In 1911 it is noted again "instructions to sell the freehold at £3,500" and in December of that year it is recorded that the house has "water laid on", which would mean flushing water closets as well as other modern amenities. Up until that point the house had very primitive sanitation and water was brought from a well situated between *Pinehurst* and *Heather Brow*.

On the 13th June 1912 it is noted in the Cubitt and West ledgers that "This is now let to a member of Mr I'Anson's family".

For a number of years after their marriage in 1902, Maud and Cyril Fraser lived at *Broxhead Warren* and eventually in 1917 they built their own house on Barley Mow Hill, known as *Barley Mow House*. They lived there until 1933, when it was sold for the first time, appearing in Country Life at the time and described as "Owner built – on the market for the first time". By this time Cyril would have been in his seventies and it may have been put on the market because of his death, or perhaps the Frasers decided to move to a smaller house. This is the last trace of Maud and Cyril as they are not buried in Headley churchyard and seem to disappear from Headley completely. It is not known if they had any children, but between the 1930s and 1940s an Ivor Fraser was living at *Pentlow* on Headley Hill Road – was this a son or relative of Maud and Cyril's?

Pinehurst, built on Headley Hill in 1899

A Next-door Neighbour

The Hubbucks build *Pinehurst*, 1899

At about the same time that the Calvert sisters moved into the Chalet, work began on a new house to be built to the west. Twenty-three acres of land had been purchased by Edward and Harriette Hubbuck many years before, in the summer of 1888, six months after the death of Edward I'Anson.

The Hubbucks had made their fortune as paint makers in the east end of London, supplying zinc paint and varnishes to the still-flourishing naval industry. Originally based at 24 Lime Street, after a fire around 1858 the business moved to a new site at the East India naval depot.

The original deeds of *Pinehurst*[12] confirm that the land was previously owned by Edward I'Anson's son, Philip Blakeway I'Anson.[13] The architect Arthur Conan Blomfield was commissioned by Edward Hubbuck to design the house, but there were three different designs drawn up for the house before the final plan was agreed and building began early in 1899. Edward Hubbuck was suffering from tuberculosis and, like so many other sufferers at that time, he sought the clean alpine air of the Hindhead Hills which was widely reputed to alleviate the condition.

While their new home was being built they rented a number of houses in the area, including *Heather Brow* which they took fully furnished from the Calvert sisters for three months, from 26th October 1899 to 31st January 1900 when the Calverts returned. From *Heather Brow* the Hubbuck family moved to *Arford House*, where they remained for the five months until *Pinehurst* was completed and they

---

[12] Now *Benifold*

[13] The twenty three acres of land sold to the Hubbuck family and the eight or so acres belonging to The Chalet, as well as so much of the land in and around Grayshott, made the I'Anson family one of the biggest private land-owning families in the area between 1862 and 1900.

finally took up residence on Wednesday 27th June 1900 with their children Rupert, Geoffrey, Roderick, Sylvia (who is referred to as 'Baby' in the diaries) and Percival.

Harriette Hubbuck's diaries of this time are a fascinating insight into the daily life and routines of a Victorian family. The comings and goings by train, up to London and on trips to the coast, are as detailed as any train timetable. Each day had a definite routine which was only altered or curtailed by the weather conditions. When the weather was fine there was always a morning walk, usually to the village shops perhaps to cash a cheque at Rogers, visit Gamblens or Vineys, the Post Office and "Mrs Noake's Bazaar". If the weather was inclement then the morning was invariably spent writing letters, often to say thank-you to neighbours having visited them for tea only a day or so before, as well as to settle accounts with suppliers and correspond with family members.

Trips out in the Brougham, the Wagonette and the Open Carriage are detailed as well as bicycle rides to Beacon Hill, Grayshott and the surrounding areas on fine afternoons. The bicycle also came in very handy in emergencies: "forgot to post letters so biked to Liphook". In one entry in Mrs Hubbuck's diary there had been a bicycle ride to Petersfield and back before lunch!

Details of servants wages and other household expenditure were listed:

> Cook – Mrs Kemp £4 – 4 – 0
> Parlourmaid – Kate Edwards £2 – 3 – 4
> Housemaid – Annie Matron £1 – 13 – 4
> Nurse £3 – 0 – 0
> Under Nurse £1 – 10 – 0
> Servants £14 – 0 – 0
> Butcher £4 – 10 – 0
> Grocer £3 – 10 – 0
> Milk £1 – 10 – 0
> Bread £ – 15 – 0
> Fish £2 – 0 – 0

"Visiting" was *de rigeur* in Victorian society, whether town or country. It was an afternoon activity all year round and tea-time at four o'clock was the social high point of the day. Headley's Rector, Mr Laverty, travelled around Headley by bicycle visiting his parish-ioners each afternoon and was a devotee of Headley's tea parties. On Wednesday 19th March 1900: "tea at Miss Calvert's 4.30" was noted in Mrs Hubbuck's diary, "the Stilemans, Mr Fraser and some other people were there". Miss Butler, Mrs Parish, the Watsons, the Beresfords and the Henslowes were other notable attendees at tea parties and "Croft Cottage" was a regular venue. On Friday 9th March 1900 Mrs Hubbuck "went to tea with Miss Hahn. The Lavertys and the Calverts were there", and on Friday 23rd March 1900 "Paid calls in the after noon starting at 2.45 – first to Miss Wynne's, then Mrs Mitchell, Mrs Hilland, Mrs Coventry. Had tea with the Stilemans. Home about 6". These particular diary entries show what a time-consuming and significant part of daily life "visiting" was before the telephone took over as a way of keeping in touch with neighbours, friends and family.

The Hubbuck family at Pinehurst

A trip to Liphook to buy a new sewing machine at Singers was a cause of some excitement, and regular trips up to London by train from Liphook are mentioned as well as the London stores visited: Evans and Jays, Gillows (who supplied all of the carpets for *Pinehurst*), Peter Robinson, Allen and Hanbury, Batchelors (who supplied all of the furniture for *Pinehurst*), Harts, Maples, Libertys and Mrs Picketts (the latter a dressmaker). On Thursday 19th July 1900, Mrs Hubbuck noted her trip up to London as follows: "The Empress Club. Left by the 9.57 and arrived at 11.30. Did some shopping and had hair done at Douglas'. Dinner at 7 and out to see *Zaza* at the Garrick".
However, fond as Mrs Hubbuck was of her shopping trips to

London, there are also mentions of jumble sales at Churt and Grayshott and numerous visits to the shops of Grayshott, Haslemere and Liphook. As well as the mundane daily events and rituals, there are references to important historical events in the diary of Mrs Hubbuck, such as Thursday 1st March 1900: *"Heard the news of the relief of Ladysmith. There is great rejoicing everywhere!"*

In the evenings there were sometimes concerts or other entertainments at The Hindhead Hall, otherwise after dinner there was usually singing and music or games of Whist, Patience and Piquet. In the summer, when tennis and croquet were played on an almost daily basis at *Heather Brow*, *Pinehurst*, the Rectory and many other houses in the vicinity, games would continue into the fading light of the evening. Tennis and Croquet parties were extremely popular and many are noted by Mrs Hubbuck, including the one the Lavertys hosted at the Rectory on Wednesday 12th September 1900 – "lots of people there till late in the evening". The very next day the Hubbucks had a Croquet Tournament at *Pinehurst*, which continued on the Friday when "Kittie (Hubbuck) and Maud Calvert won first prize – one chose a silver vase, the other a card case".

In July 1900, Headley endured a heat wave until a storm on the 27th brought thunder and rain which continued for two days. The weather dictated all activities and the ubiquitous mists which so often descend upon Headley were eloquently described by Mrs Hubbuck: "White mist in the morning, cleared by lunch – when sun broke through".

During the first half of 1901, Mr Hubbuck's health slowly deteriorated and diary entries give a picture of a different era in medicine: "Nurse put 2 cups on Ted's right lung. Afterwards had linseed poultices put on". There were daily visits by Dr Lyndon of Grayshott, who would sometimes be at *Pinehurst* throughout the night, and walks out in the garden with "Ted in the bath chair" were a daily occurrence. In fact the Bath Chair features throughout Mrs Hubbuck's diary, both in use at *Pinehurst* and on holidays on the coast at Bognor and at Eastbourne.

In the summer of 1901 another Croquet Tournament was held at *Pinehurst* organised by Mrs Hubbuck and took place over the weekend of August 17th and 18th. The event began at 11.00am on the Saturday morning and play did not finish until after 7.30pm. Edward Hubbuck was very ill, but he insisted that the Tournament go ahead and play continued through Sunday. As well as members of the Hubbuck family and their neighbours the Calvert sisters, competitors included four members of the I'Anson family, four Whitakers, Mr Laverty and many other residents of Headley and the surrounding area. Mrs Hubbuck noted that there would be about "53 for tea", and later that "Ethel and Maud Calvert won first prize". This particular social event must have been an ordeal for Mrs Hubbuck as Ted's condition deteriorated rapidly over the weekend and the day after the Croquet Tournament he suffered a massive haemorrhage and died on Tuesday, 20th August 1901.

The Hubbuck family with Wagonette

Harriette Hubbuck's diaries give us a glimpse of what was probably typical village life in England from 1899 until 1935 when she died. Familiar places are mentioned frequently as well as less familiar names: Mrs Coombes, Miss Parish, Mrs Squarey, the Thackerays, the Phillips, the Lavertys, Mrs Kingdon, Lady KB (Kathleen Burney), Lady Mansfield and Mrs Jones among many others, as well as 'Maud and Ril' (Maud Calvert and her husband Cyril Fraser) who became very close friends to Harriette Hubbuck and her family.

The diaries provide a window, through which the landscape is familiar, but not the way of life. Her daily entries allow us to see, in minute detail, how the gentry lived in rural England at this time and highlight just how privileged their lives were; a seamless routine of mealtimes, walks, social calls and visits, letter writing, sport and trips 'up to town'. The train transported them on regular days out as well as to holidays at the coast: Bognor, Eastbourne, Hastings and Bourne-mouth were just a few of the many established seaside resorts in England. Train times, connections and delays are noted with an unwavering commitment to detail and travel arrangements of all kinds seem to have provided a subject to talk and write about.

During the First World War, Harriette Hubbuck, along with many others in the village, devoted herself to the 'war effort'. As well as being a committed member of the 'working party' which met fortnightly at one of their homes, she helped to organise concerts, entertainment and refreshments on a weekly basis at the local YMCA. Every Wednesday evening at 6.30pm, 'Lickfold's car' would collect her and Maud Fraser (by now living at Barley Mow House) and usually one or two others to take them to the YMCA at Hollywater. Mrs Hubbuck was certainly a great organiser, no doubt greatly aided by new technology in the shape of the telephone at *Pinehurst*, which was used by friends and neighbours in Headley when needed, usually to call out Dr Lyndon or Mr Grenside the dentist.

Rear view of Pinehurst

During the years of the Great War the ladies of *Pinehurst* and their friends had their 'fortunes told' on a regular basis by a lady who lived in the village. The same lady also knitted cardigans for the fashion-conscious ladies in the area including Harriette and her daughter Sylvia.

From 1912 until 1923, Harriette's neighbour at *Windridge Chalet* was Caroline I'Anson[14], the widow of Edward I'Anson, who is referred to simply as 'Mrs I'Anson', and it seems that Sylvia, Harriette's daughter, rather than Harriette herself regularly visited the elderly lady next door. Sylvia would call on Mrs I'Anson, usually for tea at 3.30pm, and Mrs I'Anson occasionally visited *Pinehurst*. One of her visits to *Pinehurst* is noted on 26th May 1918, 'Mrs I'Anson called and had tea. Mrs Parish and Mrs Phillimore also', and on Sunday 7th July 1918, 'Mrs I'Anson came to tea and stayed till 7 o'clock'. The fact that the eighty-five year old Mrs I'Anson was in no rush to return home adds credence to her probable loneliness. Headley at this time was not only suffering the discomfort of 'very hot weather', but was also in the grip of the Spanish flu epidemic sweeping the country and which claimed so many lives.

On Thursday 17th June 1920, Mrs Hubbuck mentions one of Sylvia's visits to Mrs I'Anson simply saying, 'Fine and warm, a lovely day. All rested indoors in the afternoon as it was so hot. Sylvia went in to see Mrs I'Anson and had tea with her.' Sylvia by this time was twenty-one years old and Caroline I'Anson eighty-seven years old. It is highly likely that Sylvia was fascinated by the old lady's memories and tales of her life in Rome and her other overseas trips. Certainly, compared to many of the other residents of Headley at this time, Caroline I'Anson had led a sophisticated, as well as colourful life. However, Sylvia may have simply felt sorry for the old lady, living alone in a large house surrounded by the trophies and souvenirs of a spent lifetime.

Just as times moved on for *Windridge*, so did they for *Pinehurst*. Children eventually married and moved away, and the croquet and tennis parties became a distant echo of childhood and the fading Edwardian era. In 1935, Harriette Hubbuck died at *Pinehurst* and the house was later sold to a family named Squires.

---

[14] See following chapter for details of Caroline's life.

Caroline,
Countess de Champs I'Anson
Windridge Chalet, 1912–1923

Caroline Susannah Stopher was born on 1st July 1833 in Woodbridge, Suffolk to a servant named Charles Samuel Stopher and his wife Caroline. Caroline's parentage and humble beginnings are as surprising as they are fascinating given the story of her life and in view of the fact that later in life she was known as Caroline de Champs I'Anson and is recorded in the history of the I'Anson family as "a relict of the Comte de Champs". Towards the end of her life she was often referred to as the Countess de Champs, but because so much of her life seems to have been spent overseas, in other parts of Europe, there are many missing years in her life's story – which only makes her the more intriguing.

It is unknown exactly where or how Caroline grew up, but by 1858 she was living in Rome, and on March 10th of that year she married a man named James Lawrence Shepherd, a thirty-one year old Civil Engineer and the son of another James Shepherd, who was also a Civil Engineer. Caroline and James were married at The British Consulate and both gave their addresses as 17 Piazza Aracoeli. Caroline's father is named on the marriage certificate as "Charles Samuel Stopher", whose occupation is listed as "Rentier"[15].

It is possible that Caroline Stopher and James Shepherd had eloped from England early in 1858 and upon arrival in Rome were hastily married, as on the 19th October, only seven months after their marriage, Caroline gave birth to a son named Francis Woodward

---

[15] Rentier, also known as tenant in chief – a person whose income is from investments and rents and therefore does not have to work.

Shepherd at her home in the Piazza Aracoeli[16].

On 13th March 1860, Caroline gave birth to her second son, Montague James, who was also born at 17 Piazza d'Aracoeli. On 7th April 1860, one month after Montague's birth, James Shepherd registered the birth of both of his sons at the British Consulate (Francis' birth had not been registered before this time). By this time Francis was eighteen months old and Caroline and James had been living in Rome for at least two years.

The Shepherd family's home was in the bustling centre of the city, close to the famous thoroughfare Via del Corsa which was the focal point of Rome's ostentatious new civic buildings and the still-famous Grand Hotel, built in 1860. This period coincides with the very beginning of the Reunification of Italy, when there was a significant amount of development and new civic buildings and bridges were being built. However Rome at this time was still part of the French Empire, so it is possible that James Shepherd was working for the French Government, as it would be another ten years before Rome and the Papal States were fully integrated into the newly unified Italy. This was a time of unrest and revolution in and around Rome, when Guiseppe Garibaldi was mounting his march on the city in order to reclaim it as a part of Italy, and so it was certainly not a safe place for an English family to be living.

The following year, in the summer of 1861, Caroline returned to London for the birth of another son, Edward Albert, who was born on the 22nd of August. Even in the 1860s many of the inhabitants of Rome left the city and went to cooler climes during the months of July and August, as they do to this day. The family stayed at the very elegant 22 Pelham Crescent, just off the Fulham Road in South Kensington, and this was where Edward Shepherd was born. It is unclear whether this was a house the family retained for their use when in London or whether they simply stayed there on that particular visit. The family were still in London in October of that year when James Shepherd registered the birth of his new son at Brompton Register Office.

The Shepherd family were back at their home in the Piazza Aracoeli in 1862 and it was there that James Shepherd died tragically on 6th October 1862 as a result of injuries in a "fall from a bridge at the railway station". Caroline was left a widow with three sons, all

---

[16] On his birth certificate Caroline gives her age as twenty-one, making her birth year 1837 – which is a four-year difference from the birth record of Caroline Susannah Stopher from Woodbridge.

under four years old, in a foreign land. Yet despite the continued unrest in Rome and the suddenness of her new status as a widow, she chose to stay at the same address in Rome after her husband's death.

Her story becomes very difficult to put into chronological order from this point, mainly because she gave birth to another "Shepherd" son on 1st November 1863 named James Lawrence Frederick. It was Caroline's father-in-law, also named James Shepherd, who registered the new baby James' birth at the British Consulate and had the task of explaining that the father of the baby, his son, was in fact "deceased", as recorded on the birth certificate. In fact he had died thirteen months earlier – so who was the real father of Caroline's fourth son?

Cimitero Accatolico (Protestant Cemetery) in Rome

Caroline continued to live at the same address for at least another two years. There on 15th February 1864, three months after James' birth, her six-year old son Francis died. No records of the cause of his death have survived, but he was buried with his father at the Cimitero Accatolico (also known as the Protestant Cemetery) in Rome.

On 11th November 1865, Caroline married Antonin Armand de Champs, a Lieutenant in the French army in "Havre" France. On the marriage certificate Caroline once again seems to deduct some years off her true age. Her age is recorded as twenty-nine years, when in fact she was by this time thirty-two years old. She is named as "Caroline Susannah Shepherd", a "widow" and gives her Father's name simply as "Samuel Stopher". Her new husband, Antonin, is recorded as a bachelor of thirty-three years old and his Father is named as "Ferdinand Francois Joseph de Champs". Both of them list their place of residence as "Havre".

It is not known when or even if Caroline and her new husband permanently left Rome or how long they remained in Le Havre, and Caroline's life once again becomes obscure. The next known significant event in her life was her marriage to Edward I'Anson, presumably having been widowed for a second time, in the mid 1870s. However, as no records seem to be available of her third and final marriage it is impossible thus far to know when and where it took place.

It is recorded in Bryan I'Anson's book of the I'Anson family, that sometime during the summer of 1876[17] Caroline Susanna married Edward I'Anson. At forty three years old, Caroline was twenty three years younger than Edward, and while Edward had eight children from his first marriage to Catherine Blakeway who had died ten years earlier, Caroline came into the marriage with her three teenage sons: Montague, Edward and James. It would certainly have been a desirable match for Caroline, offering her respectability and security, but for Edward, marriage to someone with such a dubious and colourful past must have been the cause of some consternation within his family. It would most likely have provided a great topic for discussion among society, and one can only assume that Caroline succeeded in impressing the upright and deeply religious Edward I'Anson who by that time was very much part of the English establishment.

Montague Shepherd, Caroline's eldest surviving son, established a career in the City in "Dividends" in the early 1880s and is listed as such in the 1881 Census, five years after his mother's marriage to Edward I'Anson. On the night of the Census he was a "visitor" in Charles Legge's house at 16 Albert Mansions on Victoria Street in London. Charles Legge[18] was forty years old and also listed his

---

[17] This date is from information taken from Bryan I'Anson's book and on the I'Anson International website and may not be an exact date of the marriage.

[18] Intriguingly, more than thirty-five years later in the list of those lost to Headley in WW1 is the name of "Victor Albert Legge RFA, died 1916, a prisoner in Turkey, aged 28, left a Widow and two children now living at Stream Farm". This could possibly be Charles Legge's son (born 1888) or even Grandson, whom Edward Shepherd had obviously also known and who lived with him at his home at Stream Farm near Churt during WW1.

profession as "Dividends". It is likely that he was Montague's boss at that time.

In the same 1881 Census, Montague's younger brother Edward Shepherd was staying a "Boarding House" at 9 Islington Green. At twenty years old he lists his occupation as "Optician" and is one of 54 boarders staying in the house at that time. Caroline's youngest son James, born in Rome in 1863, is also listed in the 1881 Census, resident at The Royal Military Academy in Woolwich as a "Gentleman Cadet" of eighteen years old. However there is no trace of Mr and Mrs Edward I'Anson, either at their London address or in Grayshott, and so it would seem that they were out of the country at this time.

By the time Edward I'Anson married Caroline Shepherd he was a man of means and more or less retired (although he continued to play an active role within RIBA and was its President in 1886). Edward and Caroline seemed to spend much of their time travelling within Europe and possibly America. There are drawings

28 Clanricarde Gardens, London

at RIBA from trips to Cyprus in 1882 and 83 and one would assume that Caroline would certainly have accompanied her ageing husband on such journeys, especially given her love of Europe.

Edward had travelled extensively in Europe during his early career when he had completed many architectural drawings (now part of the collection at RIBA) and as Caroline had lived in Italy during her first marriage and for a number of years afterwards, it is understandable that the I'Ansons would have visited Italy regularly together and even enjoyed the "Grand Tour" of Europe so popular with the Victorians at that time. Rome certainly continued to be a place that the I'Ansons enjoyed visiting and had a huge influence on Edward I'Anson's work.

Their house in London at 28 Clanricarde Gardens[19], off Bayswater, was a reasonably grand Victorian house and with just the two of them living there along with a number of servants would certainly have afforded Caroline a secure place in London society.

It is impossible to know exactly how happy the union was between them, but both had suffered and endured tragedy in their lives having lost spouses as well as children and subsequently been left with children to bring up on their own. One can assume that Caroline, who was in her forties when she married Edward, would have been appreciative of her husband's ability to offer her security and a comfortable lifestyle. Shortly after his marriage to her, Edward made a new Will and refers more than once to the possibility of more children from his second marriage, so one can only assume from this that, for Edward at least, this was not simply a marriage of convenience or companionship. It may be that he was captivated by Caroline's relative youth, as well as her undoubted sophisticated European tastes, but it is also probable that after so many years of living in Italy, surrounded by fine art and architecture, Caroline had an understanding of Edward's work and interests and would have certainly been able to speak some Italian, as well as French.

Despite the fact that Edward's children were very much grown up and living their own lives, they may have disapproved of their father's new wife as he seems to have gone to great lengths in his Will to make sure that Caroline would be acknowledged and provided for after his death. The many codicils subsequent to his second marriage reflect his anxiety about her situation, knowing that he would surely die before her – and inevitably Caroline was once again widowed after twelve years of marriage when Edward died in January 1888.

Sometime after Edward's death, his mansion *Heather Lodge* in Grayshott was sold and there is little trace of Caroline being in Grayshott or Headley at this time. It seems as though she was never regarded as an I'Anson by her step-children but it may be that she, like her sons, became a guest and occasional visitor to the I'Anson homes in the area.

In the 1891 Census, Edward Shepherd (who was known as 'Ned' throughout his life) is listed as a "Farmer", which seems a definite change of career from ten years earlier when he was living in London and listed as an "Optician". He was a "Visitor" at the home of his

---

[19] 28 Clanricarde Gardens is a six-storey house with a grand entrance and is today divided into six flats – see photo opposite.

forty-seven year old stepbrother Edward Blakeway I'Anson at 28 Argyll Road in Kensington, London and was 29 years old. So it seems that Caroline's sons were by this time accepted within the I'Anson family – even if she was not.

Two years later, in the summer of 1893, Caroline's son Montague married Theresa Emilie Cazabon, the daughter of an artist and "professional singer" by the name of Vedeon Cazabon, in St Giles, London. On the marriage certificate Montague lists his occupation as "gentleman" and was living at the "Scottish Club, Dover Street" – so it would seem that Montague's city career had been short lived and that he had come into some money sometime before his marriage. Two years later, on 2nd December 1895, Montague and Theresa's son James Montague Edward (known as 'Jack') was born at Hyde Park Mansions in London. Caroline was sixty-two years old and it appears that this was her first and only grandchild, and almost certainly a cause of celebration in the family that Christmas.

However, Caroline's destiny seemed to be about enduring loss in her life and on an icy January morning in 1896, barely one month after the birth of her new grandson, her youngest son James, then a Captain in the Army, was killed when he fell from his horse while out hunting on Stonehill, Headley Down. James had been staying at Grayshott Hall with his I'Anson relatives and was taken there after his fall where he died some time later. On his gravestone in Headley churchyard are the words:

Sacred to the Memory
of
Captain James LF Shepherd R A
Who was killed while out hunting
Born Nov 1 1863
Died Jan 19 1896
I am the resurrection
And the life
He that believeth in me
Though he were dead
Yet shall live

It is curious that Caroline felt the need to state the cause of her youngest son's death on his tombstone, and an insight into the times when a death in the family still had such an etiquette to observe. It may have been that she wanted to make clear that he died by a tragic fluke of fate and not in service to his country, or words chosen whilst still in the shock and grief of losing her youngest son James, very probably the son of Antonin de Champs and a Captain in the Army. If James was the son of Antonin then his choice of a military career is poignant; following in his Father's footsteps, consciously or unconsciously. It is not known if James Shepherd was married or had any children[20].

Grave of Capt. James Shepherd in Headley churchyard

By 1901 Montague Shepherd, Caroline's eldest son, was staying in Brighton with his wife Theresa and 'Jack' their five year old son. It is probable that he was already ill and had left the London smog for the clean sea air. Two years later, on 18th January 1903, he died with his wife Theresa by his side at his home at 3 Ilchester Gardens in West London. His death certificate records the cause of his death as "Double pneumonia for 3 days, Syncope, 12 hours". In his Will, Montague is "of London and Buenos Ayres in the Argentine Republic", so he and Theresa had also lived overseas for some time. The Argentine was her homeland, although she was certainly born in London.

After Montague's death, Caroline lived close to her grandson 'Jack' and her daughter-in-law Theresa in Holland Park, London and although in her seventies she seemed to have an indomitable spirit and strength having endured so much change and personal loss. She, like Theresa, had been left a widow at a young age with four sons to bring up and must have identified with Theresa's sad situation. However, eight years after Montague's death, Theresa decided that she could no longer endure her life of widowhood and committed suicide on 16th

---

[20] In the list of those lost to Headley in the Second World War there is a John R M Shepherd – could this possibly have been a son of James', with the "M" standing for the family name "Montague"?

April 1911 at her home at 261 Lauderdale Mansions in Maida Vale. An inquest was held on April 20th and the Coroner recorded the cause of death: "Syncope, Carbolic Acid poisoning. Suicide. Unsound mind". Sixteen-year-old 'Jack' was immediately brought down from London to Stream Farm to live with Edward Shepherd ("Uncle Ned"), his Guardian.

Theresa is buried in Headley churchyard alongside, but not with, her husband Montague and close to the grave of Captain James, her young brother-in-law. On her tombstone are the following lines:

"In affectionate
remembrance of
Theresa Emily
Wife of M J Shepherd
Died on April 16th 1911 aged 43 years
His mercy endureth forever"

This dedication is most likely to be from Caroline herself. Interestingly, Theresa's middle name which was "Amelie" at her birth became Emily at her death, just as Susannah, Caroline's middle name, became Susan upon her death. Caroline chose to give Theresa an ornate headstone and her own grave rather than bury her with her husband Montague, and yet there was certainly a space left at the bottom of Montague's tombstone and one assumes that this had been for his wife's name to be added one day. It seems unlikely that Theresa had requested to be buried alone and much more likely that Caroline made this decision, maybe in anger at Theresa's suicide and abandonment of her son 'Jack'. It does seem that when death occurred in the family Caroline took it upon herself to decide how and where to bury her family, almost regardless of their wishes. She had dealt with death so much in her life that maybe she felt she knew how things should and ought to be done. Death in Victorian times had an etiquette to observe and mourning was a large part of that etiquette. Caroline had ignored her husband Edward's wishes, stated in his Will, to be buried with his first wife ("should I die in London") and it seems that she took it upon herself to decide Theresa's final resting place. This may also be a clue to her relationship with her surviving son Edward.

Caroline by this time had lost three husbands and outlived three of her four sons. Mourning her sons should have brought her closer to Edward, who remained unmarried, but this does not necessarily appear to have been the case. Edward Shepherd was living in Headley at Stream Farm, on Frensham Lane near Churt. He was Land Steward to Alexander Ingham Whitaker who owned the Wishanger Estate and who had married Edward I'Anson's granddaughter and Caroline's step-granddaughter Berthe de Pury in 1895. The Whitakers lived at Grayshott Hall at this time, where Edward Blakeway I'Anson (Berthe's uncle) had undertaken the extensive additions and renovations to the property during the mid to late 1890s.

In 1911, the same year that 'Jack' came to live with 'Uncle Ned', Caroline made the decision to leave London and come to live in Headley at The Chalet, a house which, as we have noted, may well have been built for her by her husband many years earlier. She immediately reverted to using the original name for the house, "The Chalet" as opposed to "Headley Hill" as it had been known in the 1880s and 1890s, and "Heather Brow" between 1900 and 1910. It is almost certain that Edward Blakeway I'Anson, the architect and Caroline's step-son, was involved in this decision and in the logistics of Caroline's move from London. After his father's death, Edward Blakeway I'Anson had been the head of the family and the I'Anson Trust Estates which looked after the many I'Anson properties, including The Chalet.

Thought to be Caroline with her son Edward 'Ned' Shepherd (right) at Grayshott Hall

The Cubitt and West ledger of 1912 confirms "Mrs C. de C. I'Anson" as the person living at the house and states "this has been let unfurnished on lease to Mrs I'Anson and is now called The Chalet". Here again Caroline's dominant spirit is in evidence; not for her the names *Heather Brow* or *Headley Hill* but the name her husband had given to the house when he had built it almost forty years earlier.

Edward Blakeway I'Anson[21], who had previously been listed in all matters regarding the house was replaced in 1912 by "A H Stephens Esq Agent for I'Anson Trust Estates, 7a Laurence Pountney Hill, EC". Who actually owned the house at this time is complicated. After Edward I'Anson the elder had died, the house seems to have been part of the I'Anson Trust Estate Properties which he goes to great length to explain in his Will. Edward Blakeway I'Anson, his son and heir, seems to have been responsible for the property for many years until he died in November 1912. After this time the property continued to be part of the I'Anson Trust Estate Properties, certainly allowing Caroline to live in it for her lifetime. However women still had so few rights to property at this time that it is no surprise that the house may not have ever been Caroline's to own.

The Chalet is listed in the Cubitt and West ledgers of 1911 with eight bedrooms, as well as a dressing room and a bathroom, so it would appear that the house had been added to and altered around 1911. It may have been enlarged in order to put on the market and sell, as Edward Blakeway I'Anson had been trying to sell the house earlier in 1911, or more likely the work was completed due to and prior to Caroline's arrival at the house. A new wing was added giving the space to create a spacious new master bedroom, dressing room and bathroom. As noted in the Cubitt and West ledgers of this date, "water laid on and modern drainage" would indicate that up until that time the house had had quite primitive sanitation. It would probably have been Edward Blakeway I'Anson himself who supervised the work before his death late in 1912. It was certainly a sizable house for a lady of almost eighty years old to move into, and gives us an idea of Caroline's lifestyle, tastes and expectations. From her years living in Italy and possibly other parts of Europe she had acquired some fine pieces of furniture and art[22].

Mr Laverty mentions Mrs I'Anson at the house from 1912, and once again shows himself as a recorder of detail when he notes the

---

[21] Edward Blakeway I'Anson died in November 1912 at his home, 3 Argyle Road in Kensington, London. He had never married and is buried at St Luke's in Grayshott in the shadow of the church he designed and played such a prominent role in building. It was Edward Blakeway I'Anson who was responsible for establishing the now famous I'Anson Cricket Cup.

[22] Various items of fine furniture came from Ned and therefore probably from Caroline. Jeremy Whitaker particularly recalls a gold watch, which his father had and which came from Caroline I'Anson. On the back it had two entwined back to back "C"s – for Caroline de Champs.

succession of gardeners at The Chalet. He writes about a Mr Starkey in 1912, then in June 1915 of "Moore, the new gardener at Mrs I'Anson's", then again "Champion – came as gardener 1916 to Mrs I'Anson" and "Nobbs" in 1918 – "gardener at Mrs I'Anson's". Finally, "Cordery, new gardener 1921 at Headley Hill – came from Sir Anthony Cope". One can only assume that Caroline had very high standards in her garden with such a turnover of staff, or was it that she was simply a difficult woman to please?

'Jack' Shepherd sitting on the aeroplane in which he was observer

In 1914, only two years after Caroline moved to Headley, the Great War began and her grandson 'Jack', like so many of Headley's young men, went to fight "for King and Country" at eighteen years old. Three years later, at 21 years of age, he was killed. Mr Laverty, who was noting the huge losses to the village, mentions him in his list as:

Shepherd, James Montague Edward, Flight Commander
R.F.C. Missing in France in Feb. 1917, was seen to fall over
the enemy's lines. Grandson of Mrs. I'Anson, of the Chalet,
nephew of Mr E. A. Shepherd of Stream.

At eighty-four years old, Caroline was alone at The Chalet and it seems that so much of her life involved enduring loss, having outlived three of her sons and now her grandson. Her son Edward was still living nearby at Stream Farm, but he was accepted as a member of the Whitaker/I'Anson family and seemed to spend most of his time with them, particularly at Grayshott Hall (where he is to be seen in almost every family photograph). It is impossible, given the cold facts of Caroline's life, not to feel sympathy for her despite the fact and there is evidence, often mundane, that she was indeed a difficult woman and had led a less than virtuous life.

January 1903: Flowers on Montague Shepherd's grave in Headley churchyard, next to that of his brother, Capt James Shepherd. Their mother Caroline I'Anson was later buried with Montague. Her second husband Edward I'Anson lies beneath the large horizontal marble tomb seen in the background.

Caroline died on 16th February 1923 at *Windridge Chalet*. During her final years at the house she had decided to rename it "Windridge Chalet", but it is not recorded or known why. She was nearly ninety years old and had lived as a widow for thirty five of them. Between her birth in 1833 and her death in 1923 she had lived through the Victorian era, the age of Empire, the Industrial Revolution, the advent of popular travel and of steam and machinery, and a period which saw more change in a lifetime than any other. Mobility had changed people's lives forever and populations which had been insular, operating on their own time and with communities which had evolved gently from one generation of a family to another, changed dramatically in character. Before, country folk in particular often lived their entire lives in the county of their birth. Caroline was born at the very end of the Georgian era and during her lifetime had witnessed changes so immense it is almost impossible to imagine how an individual would either understand them or embrace them.

The "Last Will and Testament" of Caroline Susanna, Countess de Champs I'Anson was made in 1915 in Chelsea, London. It appoints her son Edward as "Executor" and the person to whom she bequeathed all her property and possessions, except for the poignant line: "that the said Edward Alfred Shepherd shall either during his lifetime or at his death make over or transmit to my Grandson James Montague Edward Shepherd a Second Lieutenant in the 15th Battalion of the Rifle Brigade my jewellery laces and such of my books, pictures and prints and other articles of virtu as may have any special artistic or historic value". Her will had not been altered after her Grandson's death in 1917 and so she left her entire estate, valued at £1,868 net, to her son Edward.

Caroline was buried in the row of four Shepherd graves in All Saints' churchyard, Headley, with her eldest son Montague who had died twenty years earlier. Sadly, her name is a mere footnote on the edge of his overgrown gravestone, which reads:

In ever loving memory
of
Montague James Shepherd
Born March 13th 1860
Died January 18th 1903
Also in ever loving memory of
Caroline Susan
I'Anson
Widow of
James Shepherd,
mother of the above
Born July 1st 1833
Died February 15th 1923
Until the day break and the dark shadows flee away"

Somehow the rather awkward line "Mother of the above" seems to disown Caroline. Was she not a "beloved Mother" to Edward also? – and by being that, more than just the widow of James and mother of Montague. The humble added-on lines give no clue to the epic adventure that Caroline's life had undoubtedly been, and clearly no mention of her as the Countess de Champs or the widow of Edward I'Anson. Edward, her surviving son, almost certainly organised her burial and the somewhat clumsy lines would presumably have been written by him, but it seems that he afforded his mother no honours in death. Why was she not given the dignity of her own grave and headstone? It appears to be a humiliating rejection by him and her I'Anson step-children.

Caroline I'Anson sitting, 'Ned' holding the basket on the left and 'Jack' standing in uniform behind her.

Across a path from Caroline and Montague's shared grave is the ornate marble tomb of Edward I'Anson. It is sad that in death Caroline was seemingly disowned as an I'Anson and shown so little love or respect as a Shepherd, but could it be that Edward had discovered later in his life facts about his Mother's early life in Rome and even about his younger brother's parentage?

Caroline led an extraordinary life considering the era she lived in and, rather than an outrageous scandal, it is a colourful and compelling Victorian drama: the daughter of a humble servant, in her twenties and unmarried she fled to Rome and was married there already pregnant; she miraculously produced a child long after her husband's death; she continued to live overseas with four children and married the Comte de Champs; she later married an ageing member of the British establishment in Edward I'Anson and finally came to end her days in Headley.

The Cubitt and West ledgers of 1923 state "instructions from Mr Shepherd" on the sale of the house, and this can only be the Edward who still lived at Stream Farm at that time. The same ledgers are confusing; written in a quill and ink and with details added and altered, it is very hard to discern who actually owned the house. The "I'Anson Trust Estates" seemed to have dealt with the letting of the property for some time, certainly until the death of Edward Blakeway I'Anson which coincided with Caroline's move to the house. It is unclear who owned the house ultimately. Certainly on Caroline's death her son Edward dealt with the sale of the house, but whether this was in his capacity as Land Steward to Alexander Ingham Whitaker or as the son and heir to his Mother's estate is unclear. However, as Caroline left a modest £1,868 in her will, and bearing in mind that The Chalet was eventually sold for £3,500, it would seem that the house was never Caroline's and that she simply had use of it during her lifetime. Maybe Edward I'Anson and the laws on property at that time had ensured that it was inherited by her son.

Edward Alfred 'Ned' Shepherd, Caroline's surviving son, died on 24th January 1940 in the Stonycrest Nursing Home at Hindhead at almost 80 years of age, never having married or had any children. The simple words on his gravestone are even more poignant when the real details of his life and death are known.

In Loving Memory of
Edward Alfred Shepherd
Born 22nd August 1860
Died 24th January 1940
In his 80th year

The irony of Edward's death is that no one actually knew his date of birth. Consequently the year of his birth on his gravestone is incorrect and was in fact 22nd August 1861.

Edward Shepherd's Last Will and Testament was a badly-typed document signed by him when he was seventy-six years old, and in it he appointed Captain Leith Ingram Tomkins Whitaker as his sole Executor and left him £39,000. As well as this, Edward left some very fine pieces of French furniture which he had inherited from his Mother and the following bequests to different members of the I'Anson family:

Mrs Madeline Willes – One hundred pounds
Mary Emily de Pury – Five hundred pounds
Patricia Willes – Five hundred pounds
Veronica Willes – Five hundred pounds

Evelyn Dorothy Wigram – One hundred pounds
Lilian Florence Burder – One hundred pounds
The Honourable Mrs Deloraine Gibson – One hundred pounds
John Cecil Edward Henslowe – Five hundred pounds

Edward also specified in his will:
"I give all my jewellery and watches to Mrs Berthe
Catherine Whitaker of 29 Kensington Court, London."
He went on to bequeath all of his real and personal estate to "the said Captain Leith Ingham Tomkins Whitaker".

Thus whatever Edward I'Anson had left in his will to Caroline, and Caroline in turn had left to her only surviving relative, her son Edward, came full circle back into the I'Anson family via the Whitakers when 'Ned' died in 1940.

The Viscountess Trafalgar

Windridge Chalet, 1924–1926

After the "Countess" came the Viscountess. In 1924, the year after Caroline died, The Chalet was sold for £3,500. Having been owned by the I'Anson family for over forty-four years it was eventually bought by the Viscountess Trafalgar, widow of Herbert Horatio the third Earl Nelson's heir, as recorded in Mr Laverty's notebooks and confirmed by the Cubitt and West ledgers of the time.

The Viscountess had been Eliza Blanche Dalgety before her marriage and her family home was Lockerley Hall, near Romsey in Hampshire. She had spent most of her life in London and used The Chalet as a country cottage in the short time she owned it, between 1924 and 1925. She was 60 years old at this time and obviously made an impression on Mr Laverty, an admirer of the gentry, who drew a detailed family tree in one of his notebooks to show her relationship to Nelson. One can imagine that she would have been a figure of intrigue and much discussion in the village at that time.

It is a mystery why the Viscountess sold The Chalet a year after purchasing it, and one can only assume that either it did not suit her needs or she did not like the area. She subsequently bought Pensbury House in Shaftsbury, Dorset and continued to live there and at her home in Putney, London until her death in 1940.

Harrods Estates dealt with the sale of *Windridge Chalet* on her behalf and the house was sold to a family by the name of Catt, who also owned the house for a very brief time, selling it and moving on after only a year. There is little information about the Catts and it is intriguing that the house was sold twice in succession so quickly. It seems to have been the Catts who dropped the word "Chalet" from the name of the house, as it was sold to the Trollope family in 1927 as simply "Windridge". "The Chalet" had become rather popular as a house name in the 1920s and 30s and it may have been a touch of snobbery on the part of the owners at this time to decide to change the name of the house. Caroline I'Anson had added the name Windridge while she lived here, possibly to differentiate it from the growing number of other houses in the area named "Chalet".

The Trollope Family

Windridge, 1927–1939

The Trollope family came to *Windridge* in May 1927 and lived here for the next eleven years. In that time the Trollope children – Viva, George and Patrick – came to know every path and place for a "den" in the gardens. Viva, the eldest, celebrated her tenth birthday in August 1927 with a party at the house and the twenty-nine invited children lined up in the glorious sunshine outside the veranda for a photograph.

Children at Viva Trollope's tenth birthday party, August 1927

Patrick, the youngest of the three, celebrated his seventh birthday on 8th September. He later remembered that the summers "were always sunny" at *Windridge* and were spent playing croquet or tennis or with friends who came to stay during the holidays. Photographs show Patrick and his brother George on their bicycles, playing with their dogs, posing with their sister – always in the garden and always on a sunny day!

The children's father was Clifford Cecil Trollope who was born in 1879, the younger son of George Haward Trollope and Jessie Waller (née Gouldsmith) of Fairmile Hatch in Cobham, Surrey. Clifford joined George Trollope & Sons, Builders & Estate Agents in 1900, and in 1905 at twenty-six years old he was appointed a Director. At the outbreak of war in 1914, he joined the Queens Westminster Rifles and fought in France before going on to Salonica, Egypt and Palestine, and in February 1918 he was appointed ADC to General Bulfin who commanded the XXIst Corps under Field Marshal Allenby. At the end of the war he returned home to resume his directorship and in 1918 the company became Trollope and Colls Ltd, Builders and Engineers. At this time their work was mainly in London and the Home Counties.

During the Great War and at thirty-seven years old Clifford married Viva Marjorie Norton Dawson at St Margaret's, Westminster on 16th January 1916. Marjorie, known as "Madge", was born on 13th January 1896 the daughter of Reginald John Norton Dawson and Viva Mary (née Thomas). At only twenty years old, she was seventeen years younger than Clifford. The Trollope's first child, their daughter Viva Jessie Haward, was born on 19th August 1917, followed by a son, George Reginald Haward, who was born on 3rd May 1919 and then Patrick Haward who was born in Guildford on 8th September 1920.

When the family arrived at Headley the children were ten, eight and seven years old respectively and no fewer than ten servants looked after the family's day-to-day lives. By this time the house was simply known as *Windridge* and the original name, The Chalet, had been dropped for good. There was still a formality and routine to each day at the house and each servant had a particular rank and a very specific area of responsibility. Mr and Mrs Trollope gave daily direction to key servants, including the housekeeper and butler, as to the running of the house, menus, meal times and so on, and those instructions were delegated downwards.

During the time that the Trollopes lived here they employed two full-time Gardeners, a Cook, a Butler, a Housemaid, a Parlour maid, a Scullery maid, a Personal maid (to Mrs Trollope), a Nanny and a Chauffeur. One Gardener, Maidwell, was considered "too expensive" by Mr Trollope at £2 and twelve shillings a week in 1934.

The Servants' Hall[23], just off the kitchen, was the place where the servants were able to relax, smoke a cigarette, read the paper or simply chat and gossip about their day. One can easily imagine the gossip that would take place as to the comings and goings of the family, the occasional moans and even the internal politics of those working in the hierarchy which obviously existed amongst the servants at the house.

Servants at 'Windridge', 4th September 1927

Some of their names in the 1920s and 1930s were recalled (mainly by surname) by Patrick Trollope as follows:

    Cook: – Leslie, later Meaton.
    Butler: – Worsfield, dismissed 1931.
    Humphreys – left 1936 (to be a Steward with P&O)
    Parlour Maid: – Triggs, later Sally the sister of Humphreys.
    Housemaid: – Pride (mentioned by Mr Laverty).
    Nanny: – Spence
    Chauffeur: – Andre
    Gardeners: – Marshall, (nicknamed Tump) for 7 years until
        Jan 1934; Dedman (left May 1932); Chisnell (also
        worked as Chauffeur until 1938); Howe
    Garden Boy: – Small

---

[23] This room is now a laundry room, but still a fireplace is in evidence where a big ugly boiler sits and an incongruous picture rail runs around the walls.

The photograph dated 4th September 1927 shows the servants lined up outside the Servants' Hall at the back of the house in their uniforms, a testament to a past way of life.

Changes in season meant changes in activities for the family, especially for the children, and Patrick recalls the indoor games, so different then to now – board-games, cards and playing with his trains in the winter months. In the summer there was of course tennis, croquet, golf, bicycle rides and picnics at Frensham Ponds. One has to remember that these were still the days before television and for much of the time the children had to create their own games and entertainment. During the summer a large canvas canopy was put up outside the veranda on the south side of the house to give shade from the sun. Rattan-style furniture was placed underneath this shade so that the family could sit outdoors.

Life was peaceful and moved at a slow pace during those blissful days at *Windridge*. Patrick remembers "like most of us" that childhood summers were "always cloudless". Photographs taken

Viva, George and Patrick
in the back garden of 'Windridge'

on those sultry days evoke a romantic atmosphere. The "between the war years", had an undoubted elegance, perhaps even a decadence, which would soon disappear forever.

For many years, summer and Easter also included a predictable visit to Ogmore-by-Sea, near Bridgend, where the Trollope family had another house that they used for their holidays. These were still the days before air-travel and package holidays to Europe and beyond, days when the English countryside was almost free of the noise and congestion of traffic.   The children also had many animals at *Windridge*, including rabbits, guinea pigs, chickens and of course their beloved dogs: "An Alsatian called Solo, a Sealyham called Martin, who died in 1935 … replaced by three Spaniels: Ben, Davey and Perro. Then Jessie, a Water Spaniel, and a Golden Retriever called Dina". Many of the dogs' graves are in the garden, located at the front of the house now underneath a wilderness of rhododendrons.

During their years at *Windridge* the Trollope family spent their Christmases in a very traditional way: a tree was put up in the drawing room, mistletoe and holly festooned the house and paper chains, made by the children, were hung with balloons in the Nursery. More often than not, relatives would come to stay and the house was a busy, bustling and happy place.

Electricity was generated at this time by an engine situated in the garden, and the battery room was at the end of a passage from the kitchen to the garages. In 1934, limited mains power was installed. The Victorian boiler[24] situated in the cellar's "boiler room" still provided the house with hot water and central heating, fired up with coke. The cellar was also used to store wood for the many fires which supplemented the heating of the house, and also to store the wine.

In the 1920s and 1930s there were open fires in all the downstairs rooms and the bedrooms on the first floor, including the Nursery where the children took their meals when they were young. There were also open fires on the top floor. Coal was delivered directly into the cellar and stored there beside the boiler.

The top floor of the house was the Trollope children's domain and Patrick and George shared a north-facing room while their sister Viva had the south-facing room across a small landing. The view from Viva's bedroom would be quite different then, with mainly pine trees, very few beech trees and no other houses in view. Now, sixty years later, there are mainly beech trees and across the valley a new housing estate, Hilland, is visible through the trees. Also on the top floor was a bathroom for the children, which had formerly been a box room or attic room in Caroline and Charlotte's day, and just off George and Patrick's bedroom was an "ashlar cupboard" which was turned into a dressing room for the boys.

The kitchen at this time had a Butler's pantry adjoining it housing all the Trollope china and glass, and it backed onto the veranda with a window, long since gone. A door from the pantry led into the scullery

---

[24] The boiler still stands in its place in the cellar, burnt out, extinct and over one hundred years old!

with a passageway across to the garages. The Trollopes installed an Aga in the kitchen in April 1933 and before this time there had been an "old fashioned range" which would have been in use from when the house was built.

At this time the windows on the ground floor still had shutters and the exterior was painted white with pale green woodwork, so that the "Chalet" that Edward I'Anson had built, and that the rector of Headley refers to in his notes of 1882 as "the Swiss Cottage", was indeed still very much a Swiss chalet in appearance (see frontispiece).

The 'big room' added in 1936

In 1936 "the Big Room" was built by Trollope and Colls' Dorking Branch and the open veranda was enclosed to form a passageway from the Drawing room to the Big Room. This, later to be known as the ballroom, became the Trollopes' drawing-room, and it was here that Viva's twenty-first birthday party took place. Patrick Trollope can vividly recall the layout and detail of the gardens at this time:

"Along the length of the south side of the house was a path which ran in front of the verandah. Beyond the path was grass and a flower bed. There were steps leading down to the lower path and thence to the woods. On the east lay the potting shed on the south side of which was a small garden with the walled kitchen gardens beyond that".

The land that originally went with the house had been sold off, and the property had only 4 acres when it was bought in 1927. However, in 1931 a further three and a half acres were bought for £250. Mr Trollope decided to put a fence along the border with Headley Hill

Road and he noted in his diary, "Hardwood posts from London and in-between thin posts cut in wood 6 inches apart and wired to keep out rabbits".

The two drives into Windridge are both clearly visible in the OS Map of 1897, long before the Trollopes arrived and when the only way up to the house was from the Beech Hill Road junction with Bowcott Hill. Travelling that route, the first driveway was "the front drive" and the second drive was the "tradesmen's entrance". However during the time that the Trollope family lived here, the upper road from Beech Hill Road was established as the way into Headley Hill Road[25]. There was a five-bar gate on the front drive, painted white and usually open, with the name "Windridge"[26], but no gate on the back drive. The front driveway "swept down to the house with rhododendrons and laurel hedges" on each side, planted by the Trollopes. In front of the house was a rockery, and steps were added in 1935 as well as a path linking the two driveways. The steps are still there today and the rhododendrons Mr Trollope planted have almost taken over the entire area.

Patrick also recalls that at this time the address of the house was Windridge, Headley, Bordon, Hants and that the telephone number was simply "Headley Down 8!"

The other residents of Headley Hill Road in the 1920s and 1930s, as Patrick Trollope recalls, included the Hubbucks at *Pinehurst* (now *Benifold*), followed by the Squires who came to *Pinehurst* in 1937 and may have renamed the house *Benifold*. At *Pentlow*, to the north of *Windridge* was a Mr Poland who sold the house to a Mr Fraser, and in the house "to the east of Windridge was Schofield, a Wing-Commander and passionate about car racing". Patrick Trollope recalled that in March 1938 a fire started on Schofield's land adjacent to *Windridge* "which we helped to beat out … but the fire engine had to come from Grayshott". The land directly opposite the house, to the north, was owned by a family called Sargent who farmed the land and kept chickens and ducks there.

"Wonderful and numerous were the fir trees and the Wellingtonias

---

[25] At this time the present Beech Hill Road was called Parish House Bottom, and the present Headley Hill Road had no official name.

[26] In 2003 some trees were cleared on Headley Hill Road opposite the house and a round cast-iron plaque bearing the name "Windridge" in black against a white background was found, with a piece of wood from the top of a five-bar gate still attached to the back of it. Today it is once again attached to a five-bar gate at the house.

with the paths criss-crossing leading down through the woods".
Beyond the woods was the stream and a field, and paths leading
through the woods all the way along to the pond in Fullers Vale where
the children often played. Before the Trollopes left the house in 1938,
a hundred fir trees were marked to be cut down at ten shillings each
with a Mr Stacey who was a timber merchant from Liphook. Sadly
there are very few fir trees left in the grounds of the house today, so
one has to imagine what the house built as "The Chalet" originally
looked like in its alpine surroundings.

The Trollopes' Rolls Royce

The cottage at this time was where the gardener lived, and it
adjoined the garages housing the Trollope family's Rolls Royce and
their other cars. In earlier years this it had been the coach house,
loose-boxes and the Coachman's cottage, as mentioned in the Cubitt
and West ledgers of 1903.

The formal gardens were those immediately around and on the west
side of the house, where the tennis court was, with steps leading down
from the terrace. Patrick remembers "St Johns Wort was in profusion"
around these steps and that the tennis court had originally been
woodland, although this seems unlikely as it is marked as a clearing in
the map of 1897 and is mentioned in 1903 as a "Tennis lawn",
probably one of the first in the area. It is more probable that the
original tennis lawn had not been very well maintained and that
Clifford Trollope restored it. Patrick comments that "there are many

references in my father's diary on the upkeep of the tennis court – mowing, rolling, potash and sand etc". Many tennis parties were held during the summer months when the Trollope family lived here, until World War Two interrupted a way of life.

The tennis court at 'Windridge'

Before the Trollopes added the "Big Room" on the south side of the house there was "a large lean-to greenhouse", originally the site of a large conservatory, "which was taken down to make room for the new building and re-erected in the walled garden" where melons and cucumbers were grown. In the map of 1897 a large glass construction is clearly evident and this was probably the original Victorian conservatory.

The walled kitchen garden "allowed for all manner of vegetables and fruit to be grown. Asparagus, strawberries, raspberries, loganberries, currents (white, red and black), gooseberries, plums, pears, apples, potatoes (new and main crop), cabbages, cauliflowers and spinach. Peaches and nectarines were grown on the walls". Beyond the walled garden lay the land which was used for poultry and the rearing of turkeys and pigs.

Patrick, George and Viva attended a day-school four miles away at Liphook which was run by a Miss Skevington. The children were driven there through the quiet lanes each morning in the Morris

Cowley open car by the Chauffeur, and collected each afternoon. In 1929 George and Patrick began boarding at Highfield School in Liphook, but in April 1931 the boys left when Clifford Trollope fell out with the Headmaster (and Founder), Mr Mills. George had been very poorly with meningitis and Mr and Mrs Trollope felt that the boys were not being cared for properly. They then attended St Edmund's School in Grayshott, under the unfortunately-named Mr Bulley! Two years later George went on to Harrow, closely followed by Patrick in 1934. Viva attended a school named Hilders which was situated on the Hindhead to Haslemere road and which has long since gone.

One of the Trollopes' cars on 'Windridge' front drive

The lanes and roads around Headley and the surrounding area were quiet and relatively safe in the 1920s and 1930s, and while they lived here the Trollope family had various motor cars which at that time were quite a rare sight in the area. As well as details of household expenditure, Clifford Trollope kept details of all the cars the family owned whilst they lived at Headley.

In 1920, before the family came here and even before Patrick was born, Mr Trollope had bought himself a Rolls Royce. In 1927, the year the family moved into *Windridge*, they also had a Morris Cowley. They had the Rolls for eleven years until 1931 when it was exchanged for an Austin 20. In June 1932, after only a year, the Austin 20 was exchanged for a Chrysler and in 1935 the Chrysler and the Morris Cowley were exchanged for two Ford 10s. In 1936 an Austin 7 which the family then owned had done 33,000 miles and was exchanged for a Morris 8 Open Tourer, and a new Morris 8 saloon came in place of one of the Fords bought the previous year.

With the rumblings of war across Europe, his children more or less grown up and the rising costs of running a big house with servants, Clifford Trollope decided to sell *Windridge*, and in the spring of 1938 he arranged for George Trollope and Sons to come from London to take photographs of both the interior and exterior of the house. At this time he was commuting daily to London by train from Haslemere and it seemed to make sense to move towards Guildford and London. Mrs Trollope, an accomplished bridge player, became very involved with a Bridge Club near Guildford and began playing at an international level. (Years later she would broadcast on the radio on bridge games). Eventually, on 8th May 1938 the Trollopes moved away to their new home, *The Spinney* in Merrow, near Guildford.

Advertisements for the sale of the house at auction appeared in the newspapers on 14th May 1938 at "the upset price of £3,000", but the auction on Wednesday 18th May failed to find a buyer. Mr Trollope returned to collect plants and vegetables from time to time, and he sometimes brought Patrick, by then a young man of eighteen. A Mr and Mrs Caswell worked at the house as caretakers, looking after the property and the gardens from August 1938, and lived in the cottage until the house was requisitioned by the Army in 1939.

The memories that Patrick Trollope has of his childhood here are of "a happy time – there was always something to do and a freedom not curtailed in and around the grounds". This freedom evokes a romantic vision of a pre-war rural England, still innocent, unhurried and safe. Patrick was understandably sad to leave, sad to say goodbye to the servants who were a part of the family, sad to say goodbye to the gardens that he and his sister and brother had navigated, mapped and claimed as their own empire, sad to say goodbye to his childhood home. It would be over sixty years until children lived at *Windridge* once more.

He recalled that "*Windridge* represented stability and we did have fun or so it seemed, but then when one is young, summers are always long and cloudless". When the Trollopes left, the Edwardian era and way of life at the house came to an end, and a year later the Second World War began. The Army moved into the house and *Windridge* had a new and very different purpose.

In October 1942 Patrick Trollope married Diana Newbold and in July of the same year joined the Derbyshire Yeomanry and went on to fight in Tunisia, North Africa and Italy. He joined Trollope and Colls on 17th February 1947 and retired in February 1987. Patrick and Diana have one son and one daughter and live in Suffolk. They visit Viva regularly in her Nursing Home.

Clifford Cecil Trollope died on 19th December 1954, George Reginald Haward on 16th May 1980, and Madge on 7th September 1986.

World War Two

In November 1939, *Windridge* was requisitioned by the Army, the 60th Royal Artillery moved in and it became an Officers Mess.

According to Clifford Trollope's journal of the time, the place was "well looked after" at first. In June 1940 the rent was settled at £160 per annum and 120 soldiers were billeted at *Windridge* in July, with the Sergeants in the Cottage and the other ranks and NCOs in the house. Headley Hill Road had a Tank Station situated directly opposite and for that reason the road was properly surfaced for the first time.

Mr Trollope commented "looks awful" in his journal of December 1941 when he visited *Windridge* again. "It was in an awful mess and badly knocked about". This is when the Canadians were here, and the wear and tear on the fabric of the house after two years of occupation would have been very apparent. It was during this period that many of the original fixtures of the house disappeared, including the banisters which were used as firewood. According to Patrick Trollope, the deep grooves on the stair hand rail, still very visible to this day, are where the soldiers chopped banisters and any other pieces of wood they could find in the house in order to burn and keep warm. It is highly likely that this was also when the shutters from outside the windows disappeared.

Mary Fawcett, whose father opened the local shop Whittles Stores after the War, vividly remembers the Saturday night dances held at *Windridge* for the soldiers. She recalls that the local young people would come down Headley Hill Road to dance "the jitter bug and other stuff" to the music wafting through the trees from the house. Many of the soldiers stationed in Headley came up to the house to take their meals in the room where these Saturday night dances were held, and it was also in this room that the V-Day Celebration dinner was later held for the Canadian soldiers stationed locally.

In July 1945 a schedule of dilapidations was prepared by Cubitt and West, but no figures were forthcoming for compensation. In August, the huts put up in the garden by the Army were finally demolished and two months later, in October, Viva Trollope moved into the cottage with her three children. Her husband Major Frederick Brady had been tragically killed after the end of hostilities in May 1945 in a road accident in Germany.

On 11th February 1946, Windridge was de-requisitioned and on the 7th July 1946 the house was put up for sale[27]. Two months later, in September 1946 the house found its fifth owner when it was bought by Mr Duke for £2,500.

---

[27] The Anderson air-raid shelter is still in the grounds at *Windridge* and has been located but not yet excavated.

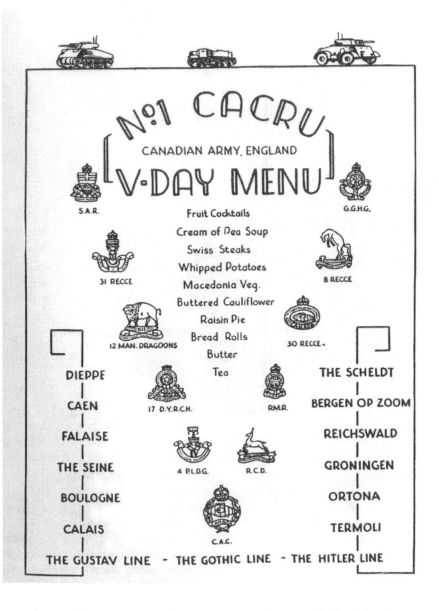

Nº1 CACRU

CANADIAN ARMY, ENGLAND

V·DAY MENU

S.A.R.

31 RECCE

12 MAN. DRAGOONS

17 D.Y.R.CH.

4 P.L.D.G.

C.A.C.

G.G.H.G.

B RECCE

30 RECCE.

R.M.R.

R.C.D.

Fruit Cocktails
Cream of Pea Soup
Swiss Steaks
Whipped Potatoes
Macedonia Veg.
Buttered Cauliflower
Raisin Pie
Bread Rolls
Butter
Tea

DIEPPE
CAEN
FALAISE
THE SEINE
BOULOGNE
CALAIS

THE SCHELDT
BERGEN OP ZOOM
REICHSWALD
GRONINGEN
ORTONA
TERMOLI

THE GUSTAV LINE - THE GOTHIC LINE - THE HITLER LINE

*Cover of the Menu for the VE-Day meal at 'Windridge' for the
Canadian Armoured Regiment troops in Headley, 1945*

Windridge, 1946–2001

The Duke family owned *Windridge* for over forty years and were renowned locally for their "bon vivant" style and for their infamous cocktail parties. However, only five years after purchasing it Mr Duke tried to sell the property and in September 1951 the house was put up for sale at "the upset price" of £6,000 at an auction at the Bush Hotel in Farnham. This is confirmed by the Cubitt and West ledgers which state "Instructed by Messrs Hewett and Lee to sell. Has been to auction – did not sell. Asking price £6,000". Intriguingly the Cubitt and West ledgers note "1952 March 10th sold by Hewett and Lee". This is mystifying, and is either a mistake or some very complicated financial manoeuvre by the Dukes at this time.

The Dukes continued to live at *Windridge* until 1991 and spent many of their years here trying to develop the land immediately around the house. In the early 1960s they tried to get planning permission to divide the house into three separate dwellings, with a further seven to eight new houses situated in the gardens. In 1966 they were still trying to develop the property and land into ten to eleven dwellings and were turned down again and again by the District Council. In fact over a thirty year period between 1960 and 1990 Mr Duke and his family tried almost continuously to get planning permission to develop the house and the land. At some stage, possibly in the 1960s, the house passed from Mr Duke to his daughter Penny Williamson and her husband Keith.

A letter from Cubitt and West in 1972 states, "Clearly, the house and cottage, as it looks now, is not a marketable proposition". This letter went on to note that the house was in obvious need of attention and that the only way to sell the cottage separately was to turn it into "one worthwhile house of ... 4 bedrooms/2 bathrooms".

Shortly after this letter was written the house was again put on the market as: "A Substantial Country House of Character in Private Village setting with Grounds Totalling about 8 acres" with "Offers invited in excess of £150,000".

The instruction was not given to Cubitt and West, who had dealt with the house for almost one hundred years, but to a new agent in the area, Gascoigne-Pees. The black and white photograph on the front of the sale particulars must have been taken on a dark, wet day and shows a sad looking place with enormous pools of rainwater across an unmade, muddy driveway and the box hedges, so beautifully manicured while the Trollopes were at the house, completely overgrown and neglected. The house looks to be newly painted, but the shutters had by now gone from the windows. The house and all of the land was put on the market without the cottage, so presumably the Williamsons' idea was to keep the cottage. Not surprisingly the house failed to sell. A year or so later, the Williamsons sold off the cottage along with the walled Victorian garden and some 2–3 acres of land.

In 1988 the Williamsons were part of a group who formed a plan to develop Headley Hill Road and build twenty-two new houses on land belonging to them. All of their planning applications were refused, despite appeals on every occasion. Subsequent to this Penny Williamson put the house on the market and in 1991 Mr & Mrs Bill Glover purchased *Windridge*. At this point a new driveway was laid by the Williamsons to ensure that the house sale went through and in order that the cottage had its own separate entrance. The new drive was laid through what had formerly been the kitchen gardens and paddock.

For a number of years, while Mr Glover worked in Hong Kong, *Windridge* was once again available to rent and a number of different people lived here until Bill Glover retired and returned to Headley. It was the Glovers who restored and added significantly to the gardens at the house, taming the wilderness of rhododendrons, laying new lawns, re-establishing borders, cutting down trees to let light in, landscaping the terracing beside the formal gardens and the tennis lawn. Certainly they restored order, beauty and dignity to the place and devoted much time to its maintenance. One has to remember that, barely 50 years before, the garden had required two full-time gardeners although since then the land had been divided and the kitchen gardens no longer produced fruit and vegetables.

Into the Twenty-first Century

'Windridge' in 2004 – compare with the 1927 frontispiece picture

In March 2001, the Glovers 'downsized' to a cottage on Beech Hill and sold *Windridge* to the Kinghorn family. For the first time in almost seventy years children lived at the house again. Max and Arabella Kinghorn mapped and navigated the gardens and woods just as Viva, George and Patrick had done in the 1920s and 30s. An empire re-emerged in a tangled undergrowth of tree stumps and fern and rhododendron. 'Dens' were re-established throughout the garden as well as a 'base camp' and, in line with twenty-first century thinking, an 'office'.

Between 2001 and 2004 extensive renovations were carried out, in order to update the house as well as to restore it. A fence was erected along Headley Hill Road, not to keep the neighbours out so much as to keep the children in!

So the house, built in the 1870s, has seen a cast of characters move through its rooms with changing fashions and new inventions, through two world wars, and has emerged into the cacophony and bright lights of the modern world. Like so many older houses which have withstood so much change it inevitably represents a continuity and even stability, but also serves to remind us of a simpler and perhaps more elegant age which existed not so very long ago.

ରେ ରେ ରେ

Latterly ...

About a year after moving in we had reason to believe that we had a ghost! A friend recommended we speak to a lady in London who was a psychic and a healer. The psychic lady came to visit us and as soon as she entered the house she commented that it was "very busy"! She told me that a lot of people had passed through the house and that it had been a very happy place for them – for this reason they did not want to leave. She commented specifically on a young man in a RAF type of uniform, which at the time made no sense to me at all. However, one lady in particular seemed to be causing our problem. According to the "psychic healer" this lady was very distressed and sat crying at a particular window, waiting for "a boy to return". The boy was a lost son or a even a Grandson, but she could not tell me which, or anything more than that. All of this meant nothing to me at that stage and I gladly allowed her to light candles and say prayers in that room, to move the spirit on. Our ghost never made its presence felt again.

Almost two years later, I discovered Caroline I'Anson and fitted her into the story of the house. I realised that she had lived at *Windridge* almost alone as an old lady during the First World War when her grandson 'Jack' Shepherd had been in the Royal Flying Corps, and he had lived with her before going to fight. He was "shot down over enemy lines" in 1917 and never returned home. Caroline died at "Windridge Chalet" in 1923.

Caroline I'Anson's grandson 'Jack' Shepherd on his motorcycle

Bibliography/Sources

Hind Head or the English Switzerland, Thomas Wright, 1898
Haslemere 1850 to 1950, G R Rolston, 1964
Grayshott: the Story of a Hampshire Village, J H Smith, 1978
Haslemere and Hindhead, The Hill Country of the Surrey Borderland
Grayshott History, W A Sillick
Headley 1066–1966, J S Tudor Jones
Around Haslemere and Hindhead, Tim Winter and Graham Collyer
Headley's Past In Pictures, John Owen Smith, 1999
The Authors Circle, Charles Bone
All Tanked Up, John Owen Smith, 1994
What the Victorians Did for Us, Adam Hart–Davis
The Victorians, A N Wilson
Kelly's Directories of Hampshire (1885–1940)
Debretts/ Who's Who (various)
The Victorian Farmer, David J Eveleigh
Directory of British Architects
British Architectural Library Biography File
The Builder (at RIBA)
The Herald (Archives)
Headley Parish Magazines 1880–1928
Reverend Wallis Hay Laverty's Notebooks 1872–1928
The Victorian Home, Judith Flanders
Eminent Victorians, Lytton Strachey
From Newfoundland to Cochin China, Mrs Howard Vincent
From China to Peru, Mrs Howard Vincent
Mrs Beeton's Book of Household Management
The English Woman's Domestic Magazine – Mrs Beeton

Various websites

Acknowledgements

It is thanks to Mr Laverty, the Rector of All Saints' Church in Headley for some fifty-six years from 1872 to 1928, that I was able to discover so much about the early history of the house and its occupants.

Wallis Hay Laverty kept copious handwritten notes on his parishioners, their activities and events in Headley during his incumbency. His fragile leather-bound notebooks are now in the Surrey History Centre at Woking, and it was there that I first read about "The Chalet" and my story began to emerge.

The diaries of Harriette Hubbuck, written between 1898 and 1935 when she lived in *Pinehurst*, were also invaluable to me and provided a backdrop to early nineteenth century Headley village life.

Long before Mr Laverty and Harriette came to my aid, I had tracked down Patrick Trollope, now living in Suffolk, and he came to visit the house in September 2002 – over sixty years after he had left his childhood home. Patrick's personal recollections and photographs furnished me with rich detail about life at *Windridge* for a child between the 1920s and 30s.

My sincere thanks also to —

The Royal Institute of British Architects and The British Architectural Library, Hampshire Record Office, Surrey History Centre, West Sussex Record Office, and Haslemere Museum Library with especial thanks to Greta Turner.

Mrs Sweeney, Vice Consul at the British Consular Section of the British Embassy in Rome.

Jeremy Whitaker, who helped me so much with the I'Anson history, entrusted me with his family photograph albums and allowed me to reproduce them in this book.

Rodney and Stephen Hubbuck, who very kindly allowed me unlimited access to their grandmother, Harriette Hubbuck's, diaries and to reproduce their family photographs.

I am grateful to John Owen Smith for his input, unwavering interest and support with this project, and also to Joyce Stevens, Mary and David Fawcett, Anthony Williams, Sue Golding, Bill Glover, Sue Allden, Mrs Marguerita Stapleton in Dorset and Philip Bergqvist for their help.

Finally, thanks to my family, especially my parents, my husband Jeremy and my children Max and Arabella.

Other books of Local Interest

All Tanked Up—*the Canadians in Headley during World War II*
A story of the benign 'invasion' of Headley by Canadian tank regiments over a period of four years, told from the point of view of both Villagers and Canadians. Includes many personal reminiscences and illustrations.
ISBN 1-873855-00-1 May 1994, paperback, 48pp, illustrations plus maps.

Headley's Past in Pictures — *a tour of the parish in old photographs*
Headley as it was in the first half of the 20th century. In this book you are taken on an illustrated tour of the parish by means of three journeys – the first around the centre of Headley and Arford, the second to Headley Down and beyond, and the third along the River Wey and its tributaries. In doing so, we venture occasionally outside today's civil parish boundaries – but that too is all part of the history of Headley.
ISBN 1-873855-27-3 December 1999, updated 2003, paperback, 124pp, over 100 photographs, plus historical notes and maps of area.

Headley Miscellany—a series of booklets containing a compilation of historical facts and stories about Headley parish from several contributors.
The Headley Society, 1999 onwards, paperback, 44pp each issue, illustrated.

Heatherley—*by Flora Thompson—her sequel to the 'Lark Rise' trilogy.*
The book which Flora Thompson wrote about her time in this area in the years 1898–1901 and 1916–28. It is the 'missing' fourth part to her *Lark Rise to Candleford* in which 'Laura Goes Further.' Full of interest to those who know the area. Illustrated with chapter-heading line drawings by Hester Whittle. Introduction by Ann Mallinson.
ISBN 1-873855-29-X Sept 1998, paperback, 178pp, incl. maps.

The Hilltop Writers—*a Victorian Colony among the Surrey Hills, by W.R. Trotter.* Rich in detail yet thoroughly readable, this book tells of sixty-six writers including Tennyson, Conan Doyle and Bernard Shaw who chose to work among the hills around Haslemere and Hindhead in the last decades of the 19th century.
ISBN 1-873855-31-1 March 2003, paperback, 260pp, illustrations plus maps.

John Owen Smith, publisher:—
www.johnowensmith.co.uk/books